Bristol
History You Can See

Bristol
History You Can See

MAURICE FELLS

TEMPUS

Frontispiece: *St Mary Redcliffe Church*.

First published 2006

Tempus Publishing Limited
The Mill, Brimscombe Port,
Stroud, Gloucestershire, GL5 2QG
www.tempus-publishing.com

British Library Cataloguing in Publication Data.
A catalogue record for this book is available from the British Library.

ISBN 0 7524 3931 6

Typesetting and origination by Tempus Publishing Limited.
Printed in Great Britain.

Contents

Acknowledgements

As a passionate Bristolian I have enjoyed the time spent scouring well-thumbed and yellowing pages of old newspapers in my quest for material for this book. I have also drawn heavily on press releases issued many years ago by a variety of local firms and institutions. But a book like this could not be written without the tremendous help of the staff at Bristol Records Office and the librarians in the reference section of the Central Library. Not only does their tolerance in dealing with my numerous queries seem unbounded, but so does their knowledge of this wonderful city. I believe that without their help many books on the various facets of Bristol history would probably never be written.

Special thanks are also due to the *Bristol Evening Post* and in particular Gerry Brooke for the loan of photographs, and to Mildred and Francis Ford for once again allowing me access to their invaluable collection of postcards of old Bristol. I am indebted to the Clifton Suspension Bridge Trust and Zed Photography for the wonderful pictures of Brunel's bridge and to Liz Lewis of Martin Powell Communications for her invaluable help with the section on the regeneration of the dockland area. Thanks are due to Katherine Burton of Tempus Publishing for setting me off on what has been a most fascinating trawl of local history.

A book like this can only be completed with the help of so many kind people like the ones I have mentioned. If I have forgotten yours, please accept my apologies. Your assistance was just as valuable as everybody else's.

Last but most definitely not least, I owe Janet Pritchard the greatest debt of gratitude not just for being an excellent friend but also for her encouragement and enthusiasm, which ensured this book was completed.

Opposite: *A Bristol icon – the Clifton Suspension Bridge.*

Introduction

There is only one way to discover Bristol: on foot. Only then can you fully appreciate the city's colourful and long history. At every turn, from cul-de-sacs to crescents and from cobbled streets to elegant squares, glimpses of fascinating and historic buildings suddenly open up. This is a city where the old and the new meet. Parts of it are changing out of all recognition as a new Bristol arises, especially around the docks where upmarket flats, offices, restaurants and bars are replacing industrial buildings.

But for all that, few cities outside of London have such a bountiful history as Bristol. The late Sir John Betjeman, Poet Laureate, said many fine things about it. He once described Bristol as 'the most beautiful, interesting and distinguished city in England'. He wrote poems and made many a television programme about it. Perhaps Bristol's rich seam of heritage should not be surprising. It was the first borough in the country that was granted county status by a Royal Charter of Edward III in 1373. It also became a city in its own right when Henry VIII created the Diocese of Bristol in 1542. Until the early nineteenth century this was the second city in the country after London. The seventeenth-century diarist Samuel Pepys said of it: 'In every respect another London, that one can hardly know it to stand in the country'. Both Betjeman's and Pepys' words are as relevant today as they were when first written.

The city's history is much enhanced by the pioneering spirit manifested by explorers and industrialists. Some names like Cabot and Brunel have been woven into our history and imprinted on every student's mind. Others, though, are still amazingly under-rated: people like John McAdam, Surveyor of Roads in Bristol and inventor of a new road surfacing material now called tarmac in his honour; George White, the transport pioneer who gave the city its tram and bus system, its aircraft industry and much more; and William Churchman, who invented a new method of making chocolate and laid the foundations of the Fry family's chocolate fortunes.

Bristol is not a city that stands still. Its face is constantly changing to keep up with progress. Despite the clatter of heavy civil engineering plant that is now laying out new roads, pulling down old buildings of stone and putting up tower blocks of offices and apartments made of glass and steel, much remains to remind us of all periods of Bristol's history. It is hardly possible to turn a corner without finding a plaque, statue or even a street name plate commemorating an event or person from years gone by.

This book set outs to celebrate Bristol's fascinating past and explores the importance of some of its ancient traditions, generous benefactors, old buildings and colourful characters. It is not a definitive or chronological history. To attempt to chronicle a thousand years in a book of this size would be sheer folly. Hopefully, this book will make you curious about some of the historical artefacts that are often taken for granted.

Maurice Fells
Spring 2006

Bibliography

Children's Bristol (John Sansom editor), Redcliffe Press, 1976.

Gazette of Historic Parks & Gardens, County of Avon, 1991.

The Monument Guide to England and Wales, Jo Dark, Macdonald Illustrated, 1991.

Bristol Evening Post, various editions, 1932–2006.

Latimer's *Annals of the 17th Century*.

The Bristol Year, Maurice Fells, Broadcast Books, 2003.

Design Control in Bristol 1940-1990, John V. Punter, Redcliffe Press, 1990.

Industrial Archaeology of the Bristol Region, Buchanan and Cossons, David & Charles, 1969.

Bristol Congregationalism, Revd I. Jones, J. W. Arrowsmith, 1947.

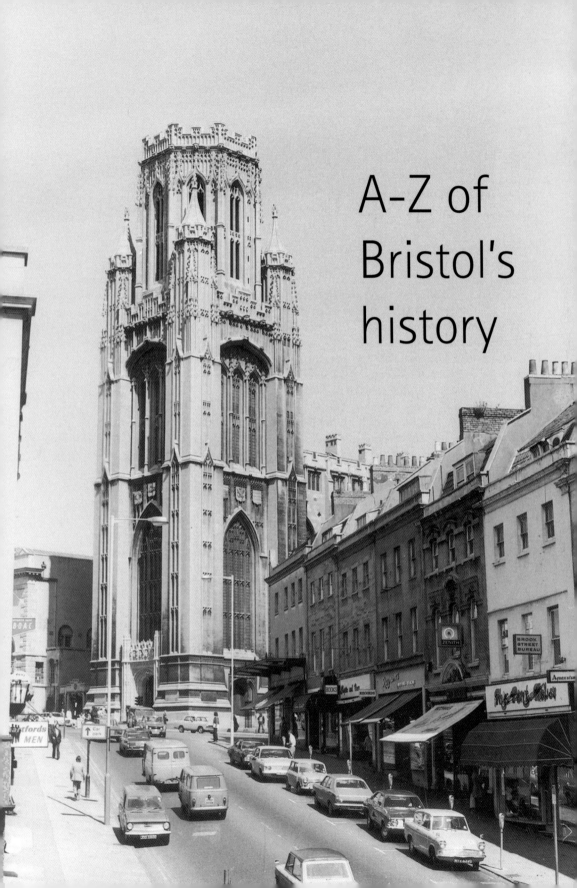

A-Z of
Bristol's
history

Arnos Vale Cemetery

If the burial records and tombstones of Arnos Vale Cemetery could speak they would give us a colourful and fascinating account of life in Victorian and Edwardian Bristol. For here lie buried some 150,000 people, including those of high office and those of no office, social reformers, pioneering physicians and inventive industrialists. It is also the resting place of many a brave hero from two world wars and other conflicts.

Mary Breillat, whose family were involved in bringing gas and street lighting to Bristol, made her own piece of history by being the first person to be interred here. She was to be joined later by George Muller, founder of his eponymous orphanages at Ashley Down; Mary Carpenter, the Victorian pioneer of juvenile care; members of the Wills tobacco family; survivors of the Charge of the Light Brigade; a policeman who was murdered while trying to intervene in a dispute over ill-treatment of a donkey at Old Market, and Raja Rammohun Roy, linguist, theologian, politician and philosopher, regarded as the founder of modern India. Amongst many campaigns he deplored the Indian practice of burning live widows on their husband's funeral pyres and called for it to be banned.

Of all of the monuments, from Gothic table tombs to obelisks, his is undoubtedly the grandest. Built of Bath stone along the lines of a Hindu temple, it has been given a Grade II★ ranking on the government's list of buildings of architectural importance. Each year in September, on the anniversary of Rammohun's death, pilgrims from around the world, but especially from India, gather at the tomb to pay homage to him.

Roy was on a visit to Bristol in 1833 to meet friends when he was taken ill on his eleventh day here and died soon afterwards from meningitis. He was originally buried in the garden of Beech House, Stapleton, the home of his host, Miss Catherine Castle. Ten years later his remains were re-interred at Arnos Vale.

At one time the site of the cemetery was part of a rather grand Georgian estate with its own mansion house. Later it was earmarked as the grounds for Bristol Zoo but its founders eventually opted for farmland in Clifton. This left the way open for the Bristol General Cemetery Company, set up by a private Act of Parliament in 1837 with capital of £15,000, to lay out the 45 acres of steep hillside between the Bath and Wells Roads as a garden cemetery. It was opened two years later and designed in the style of a Greek necropolis, using trees and plants noted in classical legend such as cypress, yew and laurel.

A number of cemeteries were later opened across Bristol, some by suburban Parish Councils as at Brislington and Shirehampton, but Arnos Vale remains not only the biggest but also the most spectacular and visually attractive. Through the design and context

Rajah Rammohun Roy, regarded as one of the founders of modern India.

Rajah Rammohun Roy's tomb at Arnos Vale Cemetery.

of the memorials it is also a fascinating map of the city's social history. Ownership of the cemetery is now in the hands of Bristol City Council, which in turn has licensed a charitable group, the Arnos Vale Cemetery Trust, to manage it. As has been mentioned, this burial ground has a Grade II* ranking on the Register of Historic Parks and Gardens but unfortunately it has fallen into a state of serious disrepair. However, various restoration projects are underway to restore the cemetery to its former glory. Although Arnos Vale is closed for funerals it is open to visitors.

Ashton Court

It has been around so long that we tend to take it for granted, but with its mansion and more than 800 acres of gardens, meadows and woodland, Ashton Court is something of a treasure. It's hard to believe that it was at the centre of one of the most bizarre court cases recorded in legal history. A judge at the old Gloucestershire Assizes in 1852 was asked to determine the ownership of the mansion and its grounds after an astonishing claim from a convicted horse thief.

The house had been home to the Smyth family for more than 300 years when one Thomas Provis arrived on the scene. Calling himself Sir Richard Smyth, he said he was the long-lost heir to the family and its estates. His story was that his father, Sir Hugh Smyth, was a former owner who had died thirty years before. He claimed his mother was the daughter of a count and had married his father at a secret ceremony in Ireland. According to Provis's story she died when he was born and he was given to a family in Warminster, Wiltshire, who brought him up.

Provis took his claim to court but his case turned sour when someone identified him as Tom Provis, the convicted horse thief, by birth marks on his face and hands. The proceedings took another dramatic twist when a telegram arrived from a London jeweller saying that jewellery Provis claimed to be a family heirloom had been engraved only a few months before.

The judge put Provis, still claiming to be Sir Hugh Smyth, on trial to face charges of perjury and forgery. He was sentenced to twenty years transportation but only served two years before he died.

The Smyth's continued to live at Ashton Court until 1946 when the death of Mrs Esme Smyth brought to a close four centuries of ownership by the same family. During this time they had acquired extensive estates in north Somerset, south Gloucestershire and Bristol by purchase or through marriage. They were benefactors, too. Greville Smyth Park, better known to generations of local families as Ashton Park, has been developed on land donated by the Smyth's in 1883. The park with its shrubberies and rose beds, bowling green and tennis court, is still a popular attraction.

The Smyth's connection with Ashton Court began in 1545 when John Smyth bought the estate from Sir Thomas Arundel. Its new owner was a prominent citizen, being an alderman and twice Mayor of Bristol. He made his fortune from exporting cloth, hides, Mendip lead and wheat to France and Spain in return for wine, iron and dyestuffs.

There have been many additions and alterations to the house down the centuries. Remains of fifteenth and sixteenth-century work have been incorporated in the

The south side of Ashton Court Mansion.

present building. The most notable feature today is the long façade of the south front, in two different styles either side of the central entrance. But the history of the estate goes back much further. People have lived here for more than 3,000 years, farming the land since Bronze and Iron Age times.

After the death of Esme Smyth the house remained empty and neglected for many years. Her grandson and heir, Greville Cavendish Smyth, apparently did not wish to live there and in 1959 Bristol Corporation bought Ashton Court for £103,200. It meant that Bristolians could enjoy this monument to English landscape architecture and to its most recent designer, the nineteenth-century expert Humphry Repton, who is numbered amongst the greatest in his field. The work of the English renaissance architect Inigo Jones can be seen in the mansion's Long Gallery and the rooms above.

Millions of pounds, some of it from the Heritage Lottery Fund, have been spent on restoring the house, a Grade I★ Listed Building, which had been showing serious signs of advancing decay. It has now become a banqueting and conference centre, whilst the parkland is home to many well-established annual events including the international balloon fiesta and the kite festival, attracting many thousands of visitors.

Names from the Smyth family live on in the naming of Greville Street and Smyth, Upton and Irby Roads, not far from Ashton Court. Although the estate is on the south west edge of Bristol only a few acres are within the city boundary. The rest of it lies in north Somerset.

Barton Hill

To the east of the city centre is Barton Hill, an area first mentioned in the Domesday Book. It largely consisted of farms and fields until 1809, when the Feeder Canal was constructed. This was followed by industry and housing.

The Rhubarb Tavern in Queen Ann Road is Barton Hill's oldest surviving building. It was originally an eighteenth-century farmhouse, which was converted into a public house in 1880, with the red brick extension at the front being added much later. The tavern takes its name from the plant that grew abundantly in the fields all around. This is believed to be the only hostelry in the country called the Rhubarb Tavern. At the back of the tavern is a stone mantelpiece bearing the carved initials D.T.A. and the date 1672. This is the original fireplace from Tilly's Court, a Queen Anne mansion that stood opposite the pub until 1894 when it was replaced by a school. The initials stand for Thomas A. Day, one of the wealthiest merchants in the city, who owned the mansion. He was Mayor of Bristol from 1687-1688.

Barton Hill's biggest employer was the Great Western Cotton Factory, which opened in 1838 and at one time employed 1,800 people, mainly women and girls. This was the biggest steam-driven factory in the south of England. The spinning mill was six stories high. With the weaving sheds and other outbuildings the factory occupied a 7 acre site. The workers lived in the back-to-back houses that packed the narrow streets nearby. While the demand for cotton goods boomed nearly 100,000 spindles and 1,600 looms were kept busy. Production at Barton Hill continued until 1925 when the firm found it could no longer compete with the mills in Lancashire and those abroad.

The Great Western Cotton Factory was eventually demolished in 1968 and was replaced by the Barton Hill trading estate. The workers' homes came down too to make way for flats. These were the first tower blocks in Bristol – the tallest outside London at the time. Barton House was the first block to be completed in 1958.

Bristol Blitzes

The first great raid of what became known as the Bristol blitzes started shortly before 6.30 p.m. on 24 November 1940. It was not until fifteen minutes after midnight that the sirens sounded the 'all clear'. The heart of the old city had been devastated, with many ancient buildings and architectural treasures being destroyed. The Germans announced that 'Bristol has been wiped out'.

Over the next eight months the German Luftwaffe bombed Bristol a further twenty-nine times. Some of the air raids lasted as long as twelve hours. On one occasion nearly 200 fires were reported. Bristol Fire Brigade was so overwhelmed with calls that it had to ask for help: reinforcements were called in from brigades as far away as Buckinghamshire, Devon and Cornwall.

One of the worst raids was on Good Friday 1941. It brought an end to the city's electric trams after a bomb fell near the system's generating station. There were many

A view of Granville Street, Barton Hill.

The Great Western Cotton Factory, c. 1900.

Staff of the Great Western Cotton Company, 1899.

St Paul's Church, Southville, rebuilt from wartime ashes.

remarkable stories of bravery and gallantry as Bristolians rescued neighbours from the ruins that once were their homes. There were also accounts of amazing escapes. A direct hit on St Paul's church, Coronation Road, Southville, left only its four walls and tower standing. Three hundred people who had sought refuge in the crypt were unhurt. Ten brides who were due to walk up the aisle at St Paul's the next day found their wedding services had been transferred to the sister church of St David in nearby Beauley Road. Determined not to be beaten, the church authorities gave the go-ahead for St Paul's to be rebuilt.

This was a church where the pews were always packed. A census of church attendance carried out by the *Western Daily Press* one Sunday in October 1881 showed that the largest attendance in the Bristol area was at St Paul's, which had 2,316 worshippers that day. The new St Paul's, which stands on the original foundations and crypt, was consecrated by the Bishop of Bristol in 1958. During the war the Church of England lost eighteen churches across the city from Avonmouth to Hotwells and from Clifton to Knowle.

At the end of the war Bristol's Air Raid Precautions Committee was given details of the toll both on human life and buildings. A total of 1,299 people lost their lives and a further 3,505 were injured. More than 3,000 homes were destroyed and nearly 100,000 properties damaged. There was much praise for the wartime Lord Mayor, Alderman Thomas Underdown. Typical of the tributes was the one from the Dean of Bristol, the

Very Reverend Harry Blackburne. He said: 'When the Prime Minister visited Bristol after one of the worst raids and was taken around the devastated areas by the Lord Mayor, few had any idea that the Lord Mayor and Lady Mayoress nearly lost their lives the night before. On several occasions Alderman Underdown went about his work at the risk of his own life, and wherever he went he brought with him a feeling of calmness and confidence'.

Mr Blackburne said that no Lord Mayor was 'ever called upon to do so much under such trying circumstances, and no man could have achieved this enormous task more lovingly or successfully as he did'. The committee heard that almost every person injured in the raids received a visit from the Lord Mayor. He attended communal burials and arranged for thousands of families to be sent away for a rest and change.

One of the most unusual plaques in the city, at the Quay Head, commemorates the fact that some of the rubble and debris from Bristol's bombed buildings was shipped to America as ballast during the war. When this unusual cargo arrived in New York some of it was used to provide a foundation for the city's East River Drive.

Bristol would never be the same again. Recovery from the war was slow. Bombed sites sprouting the ubiquitous buddleia bush with its mauve flowers could still be found across the city well into the 1980s.

Bristol Brewed Beer

The aroma of malt, barley, hops and yeast being blended together wafted across the Floating Harbour at Bristol Bridge for several centuries. It came from the brewery in Bath Street which backed onto the harbour. Although the exact origins of brewing on this site seem to have been lost in the mists of time, the names of George's and Courage's breweries will long be remembered by many Bristolians.

It is recorded that in 1702 the Mayor of Bristol, Sir John Hawkins, was brewing beer beside Bristol Bridge. He brewed a celebration ale to mark the visit to Bristol that year of Queen Anne, although it is not recorded whether Her Majesty quaffed any of it. Almost a hundred years later Mathews' Bristol Directory said: 'There is a large porter brewery in Bath Street which succeeds well in rivalling London porter and meets with great encouragement'. It also noted that the 'breweries are numerous and extensive and their malt liquors are cheaper, finer and better than most other towns'. As the number of breweries flourished, Bristol Corporation employed two ale connors. They had to taste the ale being brewed and to report to the corporation about any 'knavish brewers'.

The Bath Street brewery was the ancestor of what was to become the Bristol brewery George's and Co., one of the earliest formed large-scale breweries in the country. It came into existence in January 1788 when maltster Philip George bought a brewhouse and a malthouse in Tucker Street. By all accounts he was an industrious chap, not only brewing for his fellow citizens but also shipping barrels of porter to Cork, Waterford and Liverpool.

He took over the Bath Street brewery in 1816 and steadily expanded. George's became a public company in 1888 and started absorbing many of its competitors including the Bath Brewery, the Wilton Brewing Company, the Lodway Brewery at

The fleet of George's Brewery dray-carts at the Bath Street Brewery in the 1930s.

A detail from one of the dray-carts.

A pub at the entrance to the old Pithay serving George & Co.'s beers.

Pill in North Somerset, Bedminster Brewery and the Ashton Gate Brewery. By the late 1930s George's owned and controlled nearly a thousand pubs. A quarter-of-a-million barrels of beer were being brewed each year at Bath Street.

George's Brewery invested heavily in marketing and advertising. Many a street corner hoarding carried the simple slogan 'By George! That's Good'. George's Best Bitter became a household name along with George's Home Brewed, a bottled beer-at-home favourite. The brewery's horse-drawn drays were a familiar sight around the city.

The firm's main rival was Bristol United Breweries, which eventually became one of its subsidiaries in 1952. Nine years later George's itself was acquired by the national brewer Courage, Barclay and Simonds. Courage itself was taken over by the Imperial Group in 1972 with several more new owners appearing on the scene before the last pint was brewed at Bath Street in 1999 and production moved elsewhere.

Since then the site of one of the West Country's most historic breweries has been given over to a £150 million redevelopment project including waterfront apartments, ultra modern offices and workshops. The George's Square scheme combines bold new architecture with the best of the old brewery buildings, parts of which can still be seen. George's name can still be seen high on one of the old buildings above the Floating Harbour.

But Bristol's brewing heritage is still as strong today as it ever was, with many micro-breweries emerging including one on the site of the old Ashton Gate Brewery.

Bristol Time

Although we take Greenwich Mean Time and British Summer Time for granted, before 1880 no standard time existed in the British Isles. Every city had its own local time reckoned by the sun and signed by church bells. Bristol is just over two degrees west of the Greenwich Meridian and therefore the sun reaches its noonday peak eleven minutes later than in Greenwich.

Time didn't really matter much in a more leisurely age when stagecoaches took fifteen hours or so to reach Bristol from London. Problems arose though in 1841 when the first scheduled through train from the capital arrived at Isambard Brunel's new station at Temple Meads. It ran to what was known as 'Railway Time', based on Greenwich Mean Time. Travellers planning to catch a train leaving Temple Meads at noon had to remember it would be pulling away from the platform at 11.49 a.m.,

Bristolians were reluctant to change their time-keeping habits so a compromise was reached. Bristol Corporation arranged for the main public timepiece – the clock on the Corn Exchange – to show both local and Greenwich Mean Time. This was achieved by adding a second minute hand to the clock. Although the city eventually adopted GMT in 1852, the clock is still marking the passage of time in its unusual way.

Behind the Exchange is the only church clock in Britain with an inset dial showing seconds. The clock was installed on the tower of St Nicholas' church in Baldwin Street in the early part of the nineteenth century, with the second hand added during renovation in the 1870s. Like many other city centre churches, St Nicholas' was devastated by fire during an air raid in the Second World War. The clock's mechanism

Above: *The Bristol Corn Exchange.*

Left: *The clock on Christ Church, Broad Street, has quarter-jacks keeping time.*

25

A close-up of the clock on the frontage of the Corn Exchange showing the two minute hands.

was also destroyed but was repaired after the war and the original clock face is now run by an electric mechanism.

Around the corner in Broad Street is another unique Bristol time-keeper. Standing on pedestals above the west door of Christ Church are two quarter jacks – painted figures in the style of Roman Gladiators – who strike the quarter hours. They were made in 1728, replacing an older pair. However, these unusual figures disappeared when the church was rebuilt in 1786, enabling Broad Street to be widened. It wasn't until 1913 that they were back in their familiar place, having been rescued by George Braikenbridge, an avid collector of anything connected with Bristol.

Poet Laureate Robert Southey, who was born in a house around the corner in Wine Street in 1774, was baptised here. He marvelled at the quarter jacks and wrote of how he often 'stopt to see them strike'.

The present church is the third or fourth on the same spot since Saxon times.

Isambard Kingdom Brunel

No book on Bristol's history would seem complete without proper mention of Isambard Kingdom Brunel, adopted son of the city. Other sections in this book cover some of his engineering triumphs that transformed the face of the city but here the emphasis is on Brunel the man.

He was born in Portsea, Hampshire, on the 9 April 1806, the third child and first son of Sir Marc Isambard Brunel and his wife Sophia. After boarding school in Hove he spent two years at the Lycee Henri Quatre in Paris. The young Brunel soon demonstrated an aptitude for his father's work as a civil engineer. He assisted him in building the Rotherhithe Tunnel, the first tunnel under the River Thames, and worked himself up to become Chief Assistant Engineer on the project.

While working in the tunnel, Isambard was seriously injured during a flood there. His knee was badly damaged by a falling timber and he also suffered internal injuries. Part of his convalescence was spent in Brighton but he later came to Clifton. This was a move that not only changed the course of his life but also transformed the face of Bristol. While in Clifton he became excited about a competition to design a bridge to span the Avon Gorge. He submitted four entries and the rest, as they say, is history.

Throughout his career Brunel worked from his office in Westminster where he employed a team of assistants and a secretariat, although he frequently made site visits. His correspondence and diaries show that some appointments were fixed for dawn. Presumably, Brunel could only lead the packed business life that he did by rising early. He even found time to be sworn in as a Special Constable during the Bristol Riots of 1831 to help protect the peace.

It was not just Bristol that benefited from his vision. His landmarks remain in the stations and bridges that he designed along the route of the Great Western Railway: Box Tunnel near Bath, the locomotive depot with repair shop and the railway workers' model village, all at Swindon, and the Royal Albert Bridge crossing the River Tamar at Saltash near Plymouth.

He married Mary Horsley at the age of thirty and the couple had two sons and one daughter. Brunel died at his home in London in 1859 aged fifty-three after suffering

Brunel's original Great Western Railway station can be seen on the left hand side.

Bristol Temple Meads station, 1953. The decorations are in place to celebrate the Coronation of Queen Elizabeth II.

a stroke, predeceasing his wife. He is buried in the family vault at Kensal Green. Thousands of people lined the route of the funeral cortege to pay their last respects.

Although his many projects are monuments in themselves, there are several Brunel memorials. An early statue stands on London's Victoria Embankment. A stovepipe-hatted bronze of Brunel was unveiled on Bristol's Broad Quay in 1982, although it is being removed because of refurbishment of the area. Another statue by the same sculptor, John Doubleday, was unveiled at the same time at Paddington railway station. Family and friends contributed to a memorial window in Westminster Abbey.

Bristol regards Brunel as an 'adopted son' and clutched him to its bosom as never before for the celebrations marking the bicentenary of his birth in 2006. He is credited with transforming the face of the city not only with the Clifton bridge but other well known landmarks including the Great Western Railway, his railway station at Temple Meads, three ships, locks and docks.

To mark the bicentenary the bridge trustees installed a state-of-the-art illuminations system on the bridge, the like of which not even Brunel could have envisaged.

William Canynges

William Canynges was a medieval entrepreneur, a shipbuilder and owner who gave most of his fortune away to charity. He was Bristol's most successful merchant – the Richard Branson of his day – owning a fleet of nine ships with 800 craftsmen, carpenters, masons and seamen on his payroll, making him the biggest employer in town. The largest of his ships was the *Mary and John* at 900 tons, more than four times the size of the average ship seen around the Redcliffe wharves. The cargoes of food, cloth and drink that he sent out generally found markets in Iceland, the Netherlands and the Baltic ports but his vessels also traded in Africa.

Canynges twice represented Bristol in parliament and was also five times its Mayor. Contemporary chroniclers described him as 'the greatest English merchant of the fifteenth century'.

The magnitude of his business spread his name and fame far beyond the confines of his native Bristol. When relations became strained between England and Denmark it is said that Canynges was given permission by King Christian I of Denmark to continue trading in Scandanavia and Iceland. On a visit to Bristol in 1461 the young King Edward IV was entertained with great magnificence by Canynges at the home he built in Redcliffe Street. Records show that this was more in the style of a mansion with a Great Hall, chapel, tiled floor, courtyard and a tower. It backed onto the docks and parts of the building survived until 1937 when they were demolished for road widening.

Canynges contributed large sums of money to the rebuilding of St Mary Redcliffe after a violent storm in 1446 caused much damage. He added another level of windows, the magnificent clerestory, to make the church even more splendid than it had been before.

When Canynges' wife Johanna died in 1467 she was laid to rest within Redcliffe's walls. After her death the merchant prince gave up all his worldly possessions and

William Canynges, merchant prince turned priest.

trained for the priesthood. He was ordained in 1468 when he was sixty-six. He was Dean of the College of Canons at Westbury-on-Trym when he died six years later.

Canynges has not one but two memorials in Redcliffe church. A rather ornate and brightly painted four-poster tomb has effigies of him and his wife. An inscription describes Canynges as 'ye richest merchant of ye town of Bristow'. A few feet away is a plain alabaster effigy showing Canynges in the ecclesiastical dress of Dean of the College of Canons. He can be seen again, with other members of his family, in one of the stained glass windows. Several streets in Redcliffe and Clifton are named after him.

Castle Park

As the name suggests this was the site of a castle. Robert Fitzroy, Earl of Gloucester and illegitimate son of Henry 1, built it in the twelfth century using Caen stone. By all accounts Bristol Castle was the greatest outside London, with seven towers and a great keep. It stood to the immediate east of St Peter's church and extended in one direction towards Broad Weir and in another towards Old Market. Bristol Castle was so secure that King Stephen, Princess Eleanor of Brittany and Edward II were all held prisoner here at various times. The castle was demolished in 1654 on the orders of Oliver Cromwell, Lord Protector. The little of it that remains, including the sally-port (tunnel) to the river, some walls, and parts of the round tower are signposted.

By the 1930s this was the city's main shopping centre, focused around Wine Street and Castle Street. Bristolians promenaded here, especially on weekend nights. But all this came to an abrupt end on the night of 24 November 1940. In one of the biggest Second World War blitzes on Bristol German bombs ravaged the area destroying shops, small offices and public buildings, reducing them to ashes and twisted girders. Two ancient churches were virtually destroyed. However, the walls and tower of St Peter's, thought to have been the oldest church in the city with parts of it probably dating back to Saxon times, withstood the bombs. Its shell is now a feature of Castle Park and a poignant memorial to all those who lost their lives in the war.

The shopping centre was never rebuilt but a new one was later developed on land at Broadmead to the north east. Various plans for the Wine Street/Castle Street area were considered. One scheme featured a series of pedestrian ways linking a hotel, a museum and an art gallery to a large open space on the site of the castle. Another scheme envisaged law courts on the site but none of these ambitious ideas came to fruition. Instead, the land was cleared and for many years was used as a surface car park before eventually being laid out as a public park with sculptures, a water feature, and a bandstand.

On the north-west edge of the park a fifteenth-century perpendicular church tower has been incorporated into an office development. It is the only surviving part of St Mary-le-Port church, founded around 1170 for seamen. This was another victim of the blitz.

Christmas Steps

Hidden behind a concrete canyon of multi-storey office blocks that line both sides of modern-day Lewins Mead are the Christmas Steps, a fascinating relic of the seventeenth century. At the bottom of this quaint and picturesque shopping staircase is one of Bristol's few surviving Tudor frame buildings – occupied by a fish and chip shop. Its next-door neighbour is the thirteenth-century doorway of St Bartholomew's Hospital, where Bristol Grammar School was founded in 1532 and later Queen Elizabeth's Hospital before it moved to its present site on the edge of Brandon Hill.

The ruins of St Peter's Church, Castle Park, are a memorial to all who lost their lives in the Second World War.

Climb the forty-nine steps to the top, passing pubs, cafes and tiny shops specialising in everything from handmade shoes to stamp collections, and you will be rewarded with more history. An engraved ornate stone plaque records that: 'This streete was Steppered Done and Finished September 1669 by and at the cost of Jonathan Blackwell formerly Sherriffe of this City'. Until 1775 Christmas Steps was known as Queen Street, but was probably renamed to link up with Christmas Street nearby.

Where the steps meet Colston Street running across the top is Bristol's smallest place of worship, measuring 22ft by 18ft. This is the Chapel of the Three Kings of Cologne, believed to be the only church of that dedication in the country. It is said to be based on the shrines of the Magi in Cologne Cathedral and has the initials of the three kings (or Wise Men) incorporated into the floor tiles. The chapel was founded by John Foster, a salt merchant and mayor, around 1500 and rebuilt in the seventeenth century. The chapel has a stained glass window depicting the three kings. Foster also set up the group of balconied almshouses on three sides of a square attached to the chapel. His endowment was added to in 1553 by Dr George Owen, physician to King Henry VIII.

Christmas Steps; a staircase of shops.

Foster's Almshouse.

The plaque outside Foster's Almshouse.

Clifton Club

The architectural legacy of a criminal whose portrait appeared on a bank note can be seen in the heart of Clifton village. Francis Greenway's Clifton Hotel and Assembly Rooms, now probably best known as the venue of the Clifton Club, is still the most prestigious building in The Mall.

Greenway, who was born in Mangotsfield and brought up in Ashton, started work with his two brothers on the hotel when he was twenty-nine. It was completed just after the start of the nineteenth century with the Bristol historian John Latimer describing the grand opening event as 'the most brilliant ball ever known in Clifton'. However, one person must have been conspicuous by his absence that night.

Architect Greenway was languishing at the time in a cell in Bristol's Newgate Prison after being sentenced to hang. His downfall came while working on the hotel and another project in nearby Cornwallis Crescent at the same time. He came to grief over some creative accounting concerning the financing of the second project. This involved the forgery of a promissory note for £250. Greenway was convicted of fraud but won a reprieve from the death sentence and was ordered to be transported for fourteen years.

The Clifton Club, The Mall, Clifton.

After arriving at Sydney with a shipload of criminals Greenway wasted no time in letting the authorities in Australia know that he was an architect. Commission followed commission as he was asked to design some of Sydney's main public buildings including the Parliament Building, the law courts and many churches. The governor of Sydney was so impressed by his work that he appointed Greenway Civil Architect and he quickly soon became known as the 'Father of Australian architecture'. To honour him the government put his portrait on some of its ten dollar bills.

Greenway died in Australia aged sixty, never having returned to Bristol. Meanwhile, the Assembly Rooms became the focus of literary Clifton where writers gathered for public readings of their works. The hotel was given the royal seal of approval when Princess Victoria visited in 1830 when she was eleven years old. She was on a royal tour with her mother the Duchess of Kent and appeared before the Bristol crowds from a balcony.

A plaque commemorating Greenway can be seen by the entrance of the Clifton Club. It was unveiled on the 200th anniversary of his birth in 1977. The club has its own interesting history too. One of its founding members was W.G. Grace, Gloucestershire's legendary cricketing doctor who for a while lived in nearby Victoria Square in the late nineteenth century.

Clifton Suspension Bridge

This has been Bristol's iconic image for nearly 150 years. Its designer, Isambard Kingdom Brunel, referred to it as 'my first child, my darling'. But unfortunately he never lived

Bristol's 'trademark': Clifton Suspension Bridge.

to see it finished. Brunel died in 1859 aged fifty-three, five years before the bridge was finally completed as his memorial.

Brunel was an unknown twenty-four-year-old engineer when his imagination was fired by the announcement of a competition for designs for a bridge to span the Avon Gorge, linking the heights of Clifton with the heights of Leigh Woods in north Somerset. He submitted not one but four designs. The judges had nearly two-dozen plans to consider, including one from Thomas Telford, a Scottish engineer well-known by then for his bridges, roads and docks. But it was Brunel who eventually won the competition.

Construction of the bridge was dogged by financial crises and it was more than thirty years before it was completed. During this time the only way of crossing the Avon Gorge was in a basket which was pulled on a steel cable between the two towers.

A day of celebrations with much pomp and pageantry marked the opening of the bridge on 8 December 1864. This was then the largest single span suspension bridge that had ever been built in the world, stretching 702ft across the Avon Gorge between its two piers. It was constructed when steel was practically unknown and had cost more than £100,000. One peculiar feature is that the road level on the Somerset side is 3ft lower than that of the Bristol side. It is said that Brunel believed that the configuration of the land would have the effect of causing a level bridge to appear to be out of level. It was to counteract this that the height difference was adopted.

Building of the bridge had been made possible through the will of wealthy Bristol wine merchant William Vick. In 1753 he left £1,000 to the Society of Merchant Venturers for a stone bridge to span the Avon Gorge and said that it should be toll free. He left instructions that his bequest should be left to accumulate interest until the sum reached £10,000.

In all its 142 years the bridge has never been busier. Although it was designed for pedestrian and horse-drawn traffic the bridge was so ingeniously constructed that it is now capable of carrying around four million cars a year. It stands as a monument to the genius of Brunel and his fellow engineers and remains exactly as it was the day it opened. The huge cost of maintaining it, though, means that William Vick's dream of it being toll free will never come true.

Edward Colston

It is almost impossible to be unaware of the name and fame of the man widely regarded as one of Bristol's greatest benefactors. A dozen or so roads, streets and terraces are named after Edward Colston. There is also the Colston Hall, a concert venue, the nearby Colston Tower, a multi-storey office block and the Colston Arms public house. A statue of him stands in Colston Avenue and there are stained glass windows commemorating him in several churches. The many schools, hospitals, charities and almshouses he endowed across the city still bear his name.

Colston was born into a wealthy Bristol family in Temple Street in 1636 and traded as a sugar merchant with interests in the Caribbean. One engaging tale has it that one of his ships sprang a leak and that a dolphin jammed itself into the hole, thereby stopping the leak and saving the cargo. To this day the Colston arms consist of two dolphins

Colston Girl's School.

facing each other. Colston eventually took over his father's wine importing business. He was also involved in the slave trade – an activity now viewed with much abhorrence but at the time a perfectly legal trade. At the age of seventy-four Colston was elected a Member of Parliament for Bristol. When he died in 1721 at the age of eighty-four, the bells of churches in the centre of the city tolled non-stop for around sixteen hours.

Colston left his mark on Bristol by giving away nearly £100,000 during his life time – a vast fortune at the time – helping the poor and educating children. He is remembered with much fervour on 13 November each year, the anniversary of his birthday. There are processions of business leaders through the streets of the old city quarter. Members of the Anchor, Dolphin and Grateful Societies meet in top hat and tails at the Corn Street nails to launch their annual appeals for funds enabling them to carry on Colston's charitable works. Students from the girls' school he founded on Cheltenham Road decorate his statue with bronze coloured chrysanthemums, apparently his favourite flower. There are church services aplenty, and the laying of wreaths on his ornate tomb, designed by Rysbrack, the leading sculptor of the day, in All Saints' church. A list on the tomb records his numerous benefactions, many of them made in secret. It also shows the remarkable extent of his charitable interests.

The memory of Colston's charitable works lives on and the various institutions he founded, like the quaint almshouses on St Michael's Hill built around three sides of a quadrangle, remain to this day.

SS Demerara

The rather curious and fearsome looking figure that stares down on the city centre from high up on a pub wall recalls a shipping disaster in the Avon Gorge. It was on 10 November 1851 that the SS *Demerara*, built by William Patterson, was being towed by powerful tugs down the River Avon en route to the Clyde. The ship had been built for the West India Mail Steamship company and had been partly fitted for sea. She was being towed to Scotland for engines to be fitted.

Disaster struck soon after the ship passed under Clifton Suspension Bridge – then still under construction. Her bow struck the rocky bank of the Avon on the Bristol side and the *Demerara* swung across the river and became lodged. An attempt to re-float the vessel on the night tide amidst the blaze of tar barrels and torches attracted a massive crowd of spectators. Once again the *Demerara* broke away, blocking the river. She was eventually taken back to William Patterson's yard but by then he had abandoned her to the underwriters as a total wreck. It cost him £48,000 to build the ship but the underwriters valued the wreckage at £15,000. Three years later the *Demerara* was sold for just £5,600. Her paddle boxes were removed and she was converted into a sailing ship and renamed the *British Empire*.

Construction of the *Demerara* had caused much excitement in maritime circles for it was only six inches shorter than the SS *Great Britain*, the largest steamship afloat at the time. After the disaster the historian John Latimer wrote in his *Annals of Bristol*: 'This was an extraordinary accident which was disastrous to the most skilful and enterprising shipbuilding firm in Bristol and long cast a cloud on the reputation of the port'. William Patterson, a Scot who came to Bristol in 1830, turned out some sixty ships in forty years – including the SS *Great Britain* – from his Wapping Shipyard (near Prince Street Bridge).

The *Demerara's* figurehead – a carving of a Red Indian chief carrying a long spear – was rescued and for many years it was something of a landmark looking down from an office block in Colston Avenue. However, it eventually became so decayed as to be beyond repair and was broken up. But in the best tradition Bristol's city centre was not without its figurehead for long. A replica was carved and today it is fixed to the exterior of a public house next door to the Hippodrome Theatre.

Dockland Regeneration

Seafaring Bristol is writing a new chapter in its history, this time as a leader in the field of dockland regeneration. For this launch pad for exploration and lynchpin in developing Britain's overseas trade has captured the imagination of advocates for restoration. The transformation of acre after acre of Bristol's derelict waterside areas into a glittering showpiece has attracted international acclaim.

The quayside sheds and warehouses were traditionally crammed with barrels of wine and brandy and casks of tobacco. Reels of newsprint for Bristol's papers, along with timber and wood pulp, were stacked high on the quayside itself, a familiar sight well into the second half of the twentieth century.

Bristol City Docks were busy right up until the 1970s with commercial shipping. A bonded warehouse is on the left and railway sidings are in the centre of the picture.

An impression of how Canons Marsh will look when regeneration is completed.

At the same time a major revolution was taking place in the shipping industry worldwide as giant container ships were becoming the order of the day. These massive vessels sounded the death knell for tiny inland ports. In the 1970s it was reported that the city docks, or historic harbour as Bristol now calls it, were losing some £200,000 a year. The inevitable decision was taken to close the operation to commercial shipping, with the loss of hundreds of jobs. The disused sheds, many built of timber and corrugated tin, were left to rot and rust away, gradually becoming eyesores.

It was the demolition of the tobacco bonds at Canons Marsh in 1988 (replaced by offices) that many Bristolians consider to be the catalyst for redeveloping the area. Crumbling flour granaries have been transformed into stylish waterfront flats and houses. One shed is now home to Britain's first multi-media and communications centre, complete with cinemas and a café, while the old river police station has been imaginatively reborn as a restaurant. An art gallery and a maritime heritage centre along with cafes and pubs have also sprung up with the promise of more to come. Brightly painted ferries carry commuters and visitors around the waterfront while the old dock walls are lined with houseboats and floating restaurants. It is all brightened by a harbour regatta each summer.

Land which once formed Bristol's industrial heart and was criss-crossed by railway lines carrying freight from the port to other parts of Britain, has been bought by blue chip companies who have not lost sight of the attractions of working on the waterfront. Insurance companies, banks, hotels and leisure centres have all signed up to have purpose-built offices here. Harbourside, as this particular area is being fashionably called, will provide homes for 1,000 people and work for 5,500 when completed in 2012 in a development with an estimated overall value of £360 million. Another part of Canons Marsh which was covered with rail sheds has been redeveloped as a £97 million scheme called @ Bristol, which brings a unique combination of science, nature and the arts to life in a waterfront location.

It is hard to believe now that in 1969 council planners saw an opportunity to fill in large sections of the dock partly to create more land for roads. This was at the time when everything bowed down to the great god, the motor car. There was strong opposition from thousands of Bristolians and the scheme never got off the ground.

Cargo sheds at Wapping Wharf, where Brunel's Great Western was built and more recently a landing site for vast quantities of Guinness from Dublin, are to be converted into a Museum of Bristol.

Ships with virtually unpronounceable names from the Baltic, Scandanavia, Russia and Poland may no longer be tying up alongside the city centre streets. However, echoes of Bristol's maritime past live on at the Baltic Wharf housing estate where streets are named after overseas ports. The ships now berth at Avonmouth and Royal Portbury Docks, six miles down river.

'The Downs'

'Bristol's green lung' and the 'city's playground' are two descriptions often applied to Clifton and Durdham Downs, better known by generations of Bristolians as simply 'the Downs'. These 440 acres of open and wooded country are preserved for the enjoyment of all for ever by an Act of Parliament.

The Downs: not just a playground for people but also a favourite spot for pets.

An Iron Age camp was sited on part of the Downs and the Romans built a road across linking their port of Abonae (Sea Mills) with Bath. Ancient lead workings have also been discovered here. 300 years ago the Downs was a dangerous and desolate area often frequented by highwaymen and footpads. A gibbet stood on the highest point where the bodies of murderers were left to twist in the wind.

In 1676 the Society of Merchant Venturers acquired the Manor of Clifton, then open country, which included 220 acres of Clifton Down. Nearly two centuries later the neighbouring Manor of Henbury, which included Durdham Downs, was put up for sale. The Society agreed with the Corporation of Bristol that if it would buy the Manor of Henbury, the Society would join with the Corporation in dedicating the entire 440 acres for the use and enjoyment of citizens forever. This agreement has been enshrined in the Clifton and Durdham Downs Act of 1861 and today the Downs is still administered by a special committee comprising six Merchant Venturers and six city councillors.

In the eighteenth century many sporting attractions, from boxing to cockfighting contests and from cricket to horse racing, were held on the Downs above the Sea Walls. Racing was clearly the most popular event, bringing large numbers of spectators flocking to the Downs every spring from around 1718 until 1838. Even the poet

Alexander Pope knew of the racing and referred to what he called the 'fine turf' of the Downs. Refreshments for visitors were on tap at the Ostrich Inn, now a family home on the edge of the grassland. An added attraction for owners and riders were the trophies and cash prizes that were on offer. One trophy is among the treasures kept at the Merchants' Hall. The racing scene was vividly captured by local artist Rolinda Sharples in an oil painting of 1836, on show at Bristol Museum and Art Gallery.

The informal Speaker's Corner on the Downs often attracted big crowds on a Sunday afternoon. At the start of the twentieth century as many as 10,000 people attended meetings of the Suffragette movement.

Sheep roaming the Downs were a familiar sight dating back to Anglo-Saxon times. Not every one was happy with this pastoral scene, though. The manager of the Clifton Down Hotel on the corner of Gloucester Row and Sion Place complained that the sheep were annoying his guests with their continual bleating in the early hours of the morning. Sheep grazing came to an end after an outbreak of sheep scab in 1924. Today the grass is trimmed by mechanical mowers. Bristol University is now probably the only Commoner of the Downs still to own sheep. Every ten years or so, it ceremonially takes two sheep on to the open space. As long as the Downs remain a common (and sheep grazing is one legal proof of that) under the 1861 Act, they cannot be built upon. The sheep come from the university's farm at Langford, Somerset, home of its veterinary school.

Exhibitions have long been another attraction on the Downs. In 1973 the Queen and the Duke of Edinburgh were among the thousands of visitors to the Bristol 600 Exhibition, marking the 600th anniversary of Bristol being created a county and appointing its first sheriff.

The Downs and the neighbouring Avon Gorge are internationally famous sites for some thirty-six rare or uncommon plants. It is a place now much loved by walkers, sunbathers, kite flyers, the occasional fair or circus and a flower show. Dozens of amateur football clubs stage their fixtures in the Downs League here each Saturday, as they have done for the last hundred years or so.

The Exchange

John Wood the Elder, the architect who did so much to beautify Bath with his vision and skill, also made his contribution to Bristol's architectural scene. His most notable work in the city is The Exchange in Corn Street. This eighteenth-century public building was designed as a trading place for merchants and ship owners or, in Wood's own words and spelling, it was 'built at a very large expence …for the better Reception and Accomodation of those that are concerned in Mercantile Affairs'.

The foundation stone was laid in 1740 and The Exchange opened on 21 August 1743 amid much ceremony. A two mile long procession, accompanied by much canon fire, wound its way around the narrow streets nearby. The Exchange had cost £56,352 and Wood received a commission of £833, 12s and 11d. His design incorporated a coffee house and a tavern on the Corn Street frontage. However, The Exchange never really caught on and when the Commercial Rooms opened on the opposite site of the street in 1811 many merchants changed their allegiance.

The Corn Exchange, Corn Street.

From 1813 a corn market was held here twice a week and ever since this has been affectionately known by Bristolians as the Corn Exchange. In the mid-nineteenth century it was the place appointed for the nomination of parliamentary candidates and the declaration of polls. Election campaign rallies were still being held there in the 1960s, when it was also a popular venue for jazz and rock concerts, and now it houses various antique and crafts stalls.

Explorer's Memorial

The Genoese-born explorer Giovanni Caboto, better known to most of us as John Cabot, left Bristol harbour on an epic adventure leading to the discovery of the New World in 1497. But it was another four centuries before the 'city fathers' commemorated what must be one of the greatest events in local, if not international, maritime history. Cabot, with his Bristol-born son Sebastian and a crew of eighteen local men, had crossed the Atlantic in a small ship, *The Matthew*, in fifty-two days to make landfall at Newfoundland.

The foundation stone of Cabot Tower on Brandon Hill was laid on 24 June 1897 by the Marquis of Dufferin and Ava, a former Governor-General of Canada. He was rewarded for his efforts by being made an Honorary Freeman of Bristol. A little over a year later he was back in town to officially open the monument with an entourage of the great and the good not only from Bristol and London but also from America and Canada. There was even a string band in attendance. After opening the tower door

The replica of Cabot's ship which sailed to Newfoundland in 1997, now berthed in the Floating Harbour.

using a ceremonial key with a gold stem, the Marquis told his audience: 'We think with pride that through the fact of John Cabot having opened the door to Anglo Saxon colonisation from these shores that great people (Americans) have sprung into being'. In reply the Mayor of Bristol said he hoped his fellow citizens would always value the tower because of its memorial of the most 'remarkable historic event'.

A replica of the little *Matthew* was built in Redcliffe Wharf and sailed to Newfoundland in 1997 on the 500th anniversary of Cabot's voyage. It had been hand-built with tools of Cabot's day and the crew wore period costume. Just as medieval explorers did, the modern sailors prayed at St Mary Redcliffe before and after making their journey. The replica is now berthed in the City Docks alongside another maritime masterpiece, Brunel's SS *Great Britain*.

Cabot Tower was built with red sandstone and Bath freestone and designed in Venetian and Gothic styles, apparently to remind us of Cabot's British and Italian links. Rising 105ft from its base to the top of its ornate spire, the tower is the focal point of Brandon Hill. Those who want to admire the stunning view from the top not only need a pair of sturdy legs but a head for heights as well. The tower was originally designed with a lift inside but was never installed so visitors have to climb a spiral stone staircase to reach the viewing platforms.

Cabot Tower on Brandon Hill.

Brandon Hill, extending for nearly twenty acres, is probably Bristol's earliest public park. Robert, Earl of Gloucester gave most of the site to the corporation in 1174 and the rest eventually came into its ownership. Notice boards in the park remind us that under ancient by-laws, carpet beating and the drying of washing are allowed on the hill.

Flower of Bristol

While England has the rose as a national emblem Bristol has the *Lychnis Chalcedonica*, known locally as the 'Flower of Bristol'. It blooms in West Mall Gardens in the heart of Clifton village. This perennial belongs to the Pink family and grows to a height of about 2ft and each summer produces flat corymbs made up of small five-petalled florets.

Writing in the *Bristol Naturalists' Society's Proceedings* 1910, president Miss Ida Roper says that the flower is known to the botanist as *Lychnis Chalcedonica*, and to the old herbalist as 'Nonesuch' or 'Flower of Bristowe', while the cottager gives it the name of

West Mall Gardens, Clifton. A plaque, bottom of picture, indicates the growing area of the 'Flower of Bristol'

Fosters Rooms (left of picture), Small Street.

'Scarlet Lightning'. She adds that the first record in any book of the plant is by Ulyssus Aldrovanus, an Italian who visited many countries in search of plants and wrote a natural history around 1570. The plant is believed to have been introduced to England and Western Europe by the crusaders returning from Jerusalem.

A distinctive feature of Bristol University's academic dress is that all the hoods are University Red. This is a shade that supposedly recalls 'Bristowe Red', a locally made bright red dye in the sixteenth century. Sometimes the colour is associated with the 'Flower of Bristowe' but the flower is a brighter red than that of the academic hoods and is closer to the scarlet that appears in the university shield. This can be seen in the window above the main entrance to the Wills Memorial Building.

Follies

The style in which wealthy eighteenth-century merchants lived can be seen just a mile or two from the city centre beside the A4 Bristol to Bath Road. The striking black and white sham castle at Arnos Vale is a reminder of the days when traders seeking an outlet for their spare cash built follies. Whether or not William Reeve was trying to outdo others we will never know but his ostentatious folly included a chapel with stained glass windows and a vaulted ceiling. It was built inside one of the castle's turrets.

Reeve's mock castle dates from 1761 and was designed with accommodation for his servants, offices for his copper smelting business and stabling for his horses. It was mostly built with black slag, a waste product from his smelting works at Crews Hole. Reeve chose four acres of open countryside on which to build the Black Castle. It was opposite his home, Mount Pleasant, on the other side of the Bath Road. He linked the two by excavating an arched underground tunnel which has long been filled in.

The Black Castle was so unusual that the writer Horace Walpole, on a visit to Bristol in 1766, was quite scathing about it. He pulled no punches in describing it as a 'large Gothic building, coal black and striped with white. I took it for the devil's cathedral'.

Reeve died in 1778 and his properties were sold. Up until 1940 Mount Pleasant was used by the Roman Catholic Church as a penitentiary run by nuns. In more recent times it has been a nightclub and is now a hotel. Meanwhile, the Black Castle has also been put to various uses. Around the time of the First World War it housed an antiques business but it is now a public house. Its exterior is still intact and the chapel has been restored.

Reeve also built a colonnaded bath house near his home, where bathers could admire pictures on the ceiling and a couple of hundred plaster heads around the cornice. The colonnade was eventually dismantled in 1957 to prevent its further decay and taken by a fleet of lorries to north Wales. It was reassembled by the internationally known architect Sir William Clough Ellis on his estate at Portmerion where it can still be seen.

Fosters Rooms

The premises at Nos 16 and 17 Small Street, opposite the Crown Court, provide another link with the city's medieval heritage: 500 years ago this was Bristol's Mansion House, and the home of wealthy wine and salt merchant John Foster. He was also the City Bailiff in 1462, its Sheriff in 1474 and Mayor seven years later. Foster also served the city as its Member of Parliament. Fosters Rooms, as it is known, is Bristol's oldest domestic building and was put up as long ago as the twelfth century. Small Street was then a residential area. It was John Foster, however, who had the premises actually converted into one house at a cost of just under £7.

The building is soaked in history and when it became a set of private banqueting suites in 1961 the owners were careful to preserve as much of this as possible. During excavations an ancient well, sunk to a depth of nearly 30ft, was found in one of the three large wine cellars running underneath the old city. Ancient wine cans and clay pipes were recovered from silt at the bottom of the well.

From the 1960s to the turn of the century this was where power lunched and fame feasted at night. John Foster's old feasting room was transformed into the main banqueting hall. His study and office, complete with a large wall safe, became a private dining room and his buttery and parlour were converted into kitchens. An ominous large hook in the ceiling, once used for lifting casks up from the cellars, is still in place. Captains of industry discreetly met here to make deals over a leisurely midday meal while in the evenings entertainers who had appeared on Bristol's professional stage

The entrance to Fosters Rooms with a plaque commemorating the former mayor and benefactor.

wined and dined themselves. The first signature in the Foster's Rooms visitor's book was that of Viscount Montgomery of Alamein.

But it was farewell to feasting when the owners shut down their kitchens in 2003. The premises have been empty since then but a bronze plaque commemorating Foster, who also endowed Foster's Almshouses with its Chapel of the Three Kings of Cologne at the top of Christmas Steps, is fixed to the front of the building.

Gentlemen's Club

This is probably the only pub in the country where drinkers sup their ale beneath a circular lantern light, 31ft in diameter, covered by an elegant dome borne by twelve caryatides in the form of female figures. When the Commercial Rooms opened in 1811 Felix Farley's journal commented: 'The whole of the works and furniture are executed in the most masterly style and do great credit to the tradesmen employed'. The designer was C.A. Busby, who later helped create Regency Brighton.

The Commercial Rooms were originally funded by a £17,000 subscription from wealthy merchants and designed as a meeting place for businessmen, merchants and

The main entrance to Bristol Commercial Rooms has been unchanged since it was built in 1811.

stockbrokers to discuss over coffee the issues of the day and make deals. Its heyday was in the early 1920s when membership peaked at 1,056. However, the death knell for this venerable institution was sounded in the early 1990s when only about seventy members used the club each day. It was generally agreed that the recession had led to the decline of the leisurely executive lunch while today's decision makers were also increasingly under pressure to grab a sandwich because of demands on their time. The Commercial Rooms was the last of three businessmen's clubs in the area to close. The Bristol Club, on the opposite side of Corn Street and the Constitutional Club around the corner in Marsh Street, said a final goodbye to their members during the 1980s.

When the Commercial Rooms closed as a club in 1994 a national pub developer spent £1m refurbishing the building but retained its original features along with the name. Pints of ale are now pulled at a horseshoe-shaped bar in what was the Grand

Coffee Room. Above the bar is a wind vane which indicated to businessmen whether or not it was safe for their ships to negotiate the tricky and treacherous bends of the Avon Gorge. It was here that the first telegraph office in Bristol was set up in February 1852 when the line from London to the west was completed. This major advance in communications meant that the man who rode on horseback from Avonmouth Docks to Bristol with shipping news for members was now redundant. The club was one of the first buildings in the city to be lit by gas – and the lamps still work.

Drinkers can study the names of all the treasurers, secretaries and presidents of the Commercial Rooms – most of them eminent professional men – which appear in gold leaf on three large wall boards. John Loudon McAdam, inventor of the black stuff used to surface roads, and one-time surveyor to the Bristol Turnpike Trust, heads the presidential board. He was living in Clifton when the 'Rooms', as members affectionately called their club, opened.

This has to be one of Bristol's finest Georgian buildings both inside and out and adds to the architectural grandeur of Corn Street. At the main entrance is a portico of the Grecian ionic order supporting a pediment surmounted by three statues personifying the City, Commerce and Navigation. There is also an alto-relief representing Britannia with Neptune and Minerva receiving tributes from the four quarters of the world.

St George's

Perched on the edge of Brandon Hill, crowned by Cabot Tower, is St George's, one of two remaining 'Waterloo churches' in the country. To be strictly accurate though, it is no longer a place of worship. Bread and wine were last proffered to the congregation here in 1984.

St George's church in Great George Street was built in 1823 in thanksgiving for the Duke of Wellington's victory over Napoleon at the Battle of Waterloo eight years earlier. The location was chosen because of the growing population nearby. Sir Robert Smirke, one of three Crown architects who were commissioned to design seven 'Waterloo' churches around the country, drew up the plans. He made good use of the sloping site by creating a dramatic flight of steps on the Great George Street side of the church. Its crypt was so large that nearly 300 people were able to seek refuge there during the nightly air raids of the Second World War.

St George's was probably best-known as a church during the forty-five years from 1930 when Canon Percy Gay was its vicar. He was so popular that twenty-two organisations ranging from mariners to actors enlisted him as their padre. Canon Gay was also much in demand across the city as an after-dinner speaker.

The church was threatened with permanent closure by the Bishop of Bristol, the Rt Revd Oliver Tomkins, at Easter 1966. Its poor structural condition rendered the building unsafe and it seemed that the cost of repairs to a sagging roof and bulging wall was prohibitive. But Canon Gay was not a man easily deterred by crumbling fabric. He prepared a restoration scheme and appealed to Bristolians for £5,000 for emergency repairs. Their generosity was such that three times that amount poured in and six months later the church was reopened.

St George's Church, Brandon Hill, with Canon Percy Gay.

The death of Canon Gay in 1975 at the age of eighty-four coincided with a dwindling congregation. Many of the houses around St George's church were being converted into offices and the church never flourished again. It was finally declared redundant as a place of worship in 1984.

But a new use for the building was on the horizon. St George's Music Trust was formed to promote the development of the church for the performance of music. Being acoustically perfect the church is now one of Britain's loveliest chamber concert halls and simply known as St George's. Performances by some of the world's greatest musicians are regularly broadcast from here by the BBC.

Glassmaking

The base of a glass cone imaginatively incorporated into a hotel restaurant at Redcliffe is the sole survivor of the glasshouse cones that once dominated the local skyline. Glass blowing in Bristol was well established by the middle of the seventeenth century, so much so that the poet Alexander Pope described the cones as 'twenty odd pyramids smoking over the town'. Most of them were in the Redcliffe and Temple parishes although there was one in Bedminster and another in Hotwells.

The glass blowers of Bristol were among the country's chief producers of glass for windows, bottles and ornamental glassware. The city became world renowned for its Bristol Blue glass. Other types of blue glass had been made in Britain but it was not until the second half of the eighteenth century that fashion and the tax on clear 'flint' glass brought this particular colour into prominence with its soft rich hue. This was achieved by combining the finest Saxon smalt, an ingredient derived from cobalt oxide, with English lead glass. Although the Romans and Egyptians showed great skill in their use of metallic oxides to colour glass it was in the cones at Bristol that cobalt oxide was first added to lead glass.

After the demise of glass blowing in Bristol on a large scale, the Redcliffe cone became part of the H & T Proctor factory from 1812 until the 1960s, where chemicals and artificial fertilisers were manufactured.

Until 1930 the cone stood at over 100ft but the upper part was removed when it became unsafe. The remnant of the cone became part of the hotel in the late sixties.

SS Great Britain

Although he was a man of great vision little could Isambard Brunel have dreamt that more than 150 years after the launch of his SS *Great Britain* people would still be walking up the gang plank, not as passengers bound for New York or Australia but to admire the work of an engineering genius who pioneered modern steamship design.

The SS *Great Britain* is back in her original birthplace after ploughing through one million ocean miles in a working life which spanned nearly one hundred years. Apart from making headlines herself – this was the world's first iron steamship and the world's

The SS Great Britain in her original berth.

biggest ship at the time of its launch – the SS *Great Britain* was a silent witness to many chapters of international history.

Although the SS *Great Britain* started life as a luxury transatlantic passenger liner she was conscripted by the British government as a troop ship during the Crimean War. It was adapted to carry more than 1,600 infantry and thirty horses. More military service followed in 1858 with six months trooping, this time in the Indian Mutiny. Three years later Brunel's ship carried the first ever English cricket team to tour Australia. This was not an 'official' England touring side as we would know it today but included players from the All-England XI and the United England XI. The voyage to Melbourne took just over two months and the ticket price was a touch over £73. Two years later the ship took the second England touring party to Australia. The team included Mr E.M. Grace, brother of the legendary Gloucestershire and England player, Dr W.G. Grace. More than 15,000 emigrants to Australia arrived there by courtesy of the SS *Great Britain*. Her working life ended as a floating warehouse for storing wool and coal before being beached at Sparrow Cove near Port Stanley in the Falkland Islands in 1937.

But this remarkable story does not end there. A recovery group was formed to re-float the ship and bring her back home. An ambitious salvage operation led by a naval architect was launched in 1970 when the hulk of the SS *Great Britain* was lifted onto a submersible pontoon. The ship then began an eight week voyage home, being towed by a tug 9,000 nautical miles across the Atlantic Ocean. An estimated 100,000 people lined every available vantage point in and around the Avon Gorge as the SS *Great Britain* was towed under another of Brunel's creations, the Clifton Suspension Bridge. It was 127 years to the day after she was launched by Prince Albert. This was the last leg of voyage number forty-seven, which would see the SS *Great Britain* safely back in her original birthplace.

Since then many millions of pounds have been spent on restoring the famous ship, which is said will save her for another 100 years. It is the only surviving ship designed by Brunel and has become a treasured tourist attraction in Bristol City Docks.

Great Western Steamship Hotel

One would have thought that designing bridges, ships and a railway would be enough work for any one man. But to Brunel's impressive catalogue of achievements must be added a hotel, the façade of which still stands although it nearly fell into the mouth of the bulldozer.

His Great Western Steamship Hotel, built as an integral part of the trip from London to New York, had been identified for demolition in 1965. A development company submitted plans to Bristol City Council to demolish it and erect in its place a 100ft high tower block with offices, a banqueting and conference centre and a multi-storey car park. The scheme attracted strong opposition from a group of amenity societies and Brunel's hotel was eventually added to the government's Grade II★ list of buildings of architectural or historical interest.

Brunel worked with Richard Shackleton Pope, a Bristol architect, between 1837 and 1839 to create the hotel with classical façade, ionic colonnade, Corinthian columns and pavilions. Special features included an arched entrance to the hotel's covered 200ft long amphitheatre which provided ample accommodation for horse-drawn coaches, along with stabling. Brunel intended his hotel to be a luxurious overnight stopping place for those who were travelling to Bristol on his Great Western Railway en route to join his Great Western steamship for the voyage to the 'New World'. This was an ambitious attempt at an integrated transport system with one company providing the various forms of transport for the entire journey to North America.

However, Bristol's bid for the lucrative transatlantic trade was a flop and the hotel has since had a somewhat chequered life. It has variously been a private home, a coachworks and a lodging place for airline pilots resting there between flights over the transatlantic route from their air base at Filton. There was even a time when Brunel House, as it is now known, was run as a Turkish Bath. It currently provides office space for the city council's Planning Department.

The façade and the amphitheatre are the only remains of Brunel's original building but visitors may find difficulty in locating it, for only an inconspicuous plaque on the side of the wall records its history. The amphitheatre has life-size statues of a man and a horse, cast when Brunel House was given an extensive refurbishment in 1984. They recall the days when horse sales were held here. Hanging gardens were added to the rear of the amphitheatre when this was a Hydro Hotel. These features highlight an

THE HYDRO

END OF COLLEGE GREEN, BRISTOL.

Brunel's Great Western Steamship Hotel, pictured when it was a hydro. The façade still exists.

otherwise drab St George's Road. Although it is virtually a stone's throw away from the hustle and bustle of the city centre, this bit of Brunel history is probably a closed book to many Bristolians.

High Cross

Stand at the junction of Corn Street, High Street, Wine Street and Broad Street and you are at the ancient city centre. It was here that the High Cross, a city landmark for more than 500 years, stood. It marked the granting of a charter by Edward III in 1373 giving Bristol the status of a county with its own sheriff and separating it from the adjoining counties of Gloucestershire to the north and Somerset to the south. It meant that Bristol had more independence in running its own affairs and in legal matters decisions could be made without referring back to the King every time. Until then those living north of the river had to go to Gloucester to deal with legal affairs and people living south of the river went to Ilchester.

Bristol had provided the King with ships and men for the wars in France and the 1373 charter was given in appreciation of this. The High Cross soon became the location for civic proclamations. This was a brightly painted and gilded monument which incorporated statues of four medieval kings who had granted charters to Bristol. Effigies of a further four monarchs were added when the cross was restored and given

THE CROSS, COLLEGE GREEN, BRISTOL.

Right: *Bristol High Cross, pictured when it dominated College Green.*

Below: *A view of the original High Cross.*

Above: *A summer view of College Green and the replica High Cross.*

Left: *The replica High Cross on College Green.*

extra height in 1633. A century later it was removed to College Green – a triangular piece of grassland leased to the council by the Dean and Chapter of Bristol Cathedral – after people living nearby complained that it was a 'ruinous and superstitious relick which is at present a public nuisance on account of hazardous condition'. It was also said to be 'impeding the passage of traffic'. Even at its new location the cross still attracted complaints – this time that it was blocking a footpath. It was taken down again and stored in bits in a cloister in Bristol Cathedral.

However, in an over-generous moment the Dean of Bristol, Dr Cutts Barton, gave the cross to his friend Henry Hoare, who re-erected it on his estate at Stourhead Park in Wiltshire. It has stood there since 1768, and is now maintained by the National Trust. However, all was not lost, for Bristol has a replica of the High Cross which was commissioned in 1851. John Norton, a local architect, was faithful to the original in keeping to its medieval style and filling the niches with statues of Stuart and Tudor monarchs. It was initially sited at the eastern end of College Green but after forty years was moved a few yards to make way for the statue of Queen Victoria. It remained undisturbed until 1950 when the lowering of College Green necessitated its removal. It was then dumped in a builder's yard and left to crumble.

Six years later it made the local headlines when the city council said it was willing to give the remnants to anyone who cared to collect them in return for £50. This triggered several conservation and amenity societies to set up a fund to restore the monument. Their efforts paid off and the top part of the cross can now be seen in a corner of the communal garden in Berkeley Square in Clifton, although it is partly obscured by shrubbery.

High Finance

As Bristol's influence as a trading centre spread both at home and abroad, thanks mainly to its port, banks in the city flourished and expanded. On the 1 August 1750 the first bank in Bristol, and indeed in the West of England, opened for business. Formed under a proper Deed of Partnership the Bristol Bank, as it was called, opened an office in Broad Street and began issuing its own notes. Shortly after the turn of the century Bristolians were spoilt for choice with thirteen banks ready to help them with their financial affairs, the largest number to be open at any one time. In all, thirty-five banks offered their services between 1750 and 1900. The Bank of England regarded Bristol as an important commercial and trading centre so it too opened a branch in the city. Some of the banks quickly disappeared; others were taken over while more crashed.

For around 250 years the banks were mostly clustered around Corn Street, making it the centre of the city's commerce, banking and insurance world. Wealthy people lived here too, and the district became Bristol's answer to London's Lombard Street. During the second half of the twentieth century more consolidation followed as the names of long-established banks like Williams and Glyn's, Martin's Bank, National Provincial and the Westminster disappeared from the high street in takeover after takeover. By the millennium many of the financial institutions moved to a new commercial quarter being built at Temple Quay. The large and ornate banking halls of Corn Street lent themselves to an explosion of bars, clubs and gourmet dining.

Lloyds TSB, Corn Street, the site of much history.

A notable banking failure was that of the West of England and South Wales District Bank, which folded with debts of £5 million 'owing to large and imprudent advances on unrealisable securities'. The bank had twenty-seven branches either side of the Bristol Channel including one in Corn Street. This was built between 1854 and 1857 in an opulent Venetian style, copying St Mark's Library, Venice. Its Greek façade, with sculpted figures and magnificent friezes, is still one of Corn Street's architectural gems. It was built at a cost of £40,000. When the bank failed in 1878 the building was taken over by Lloyds Bank which still trades there. Extensive cleaning of the exterior in recent years has highlighted the splendid stonework.

Hope Chapel

Lady Henrietta Hope made a permanent mark in Bristol when she visited the Hotwell Spa. She founded a chapel which two centuries later is still being used for prayer and praise. Lady Hope, who lived near Edinburgh, was travelling around with her friend Lady Glenorchy taking the waters for healthy living and arrived at Hotwells in 1785 when the spa was enjoying its heyday.

Hope Chapel on Hope Chapel Hill, Hotwells.

One of her keen interests was that of promoting the cause of religion and she endowed a number of churches across the country. She decided to build one at Hotwells but died on New Year's Day in 1786 before work had started. Lady Hope left £2,500 in her will for the project to go ahead and Lady Glenorchy started to make the dream come true. However, she too did not live long enough to see the chapel completed. That task fell to her executors, and Hope Chapel was ready for its first service in August 1788 with room for 900 worshippers. The remains of Lady Hope were placed in the vault beneath the chapel.

Visiting non-conformist ministers and Anglican priests shared the pulpit until 1820 when a resident minister was appointed. To cope with the increasing number of people moving into Clifton and Hotwells the Hope Chapel was enlarged in 1838. By the 1960s the clergy were ministering to a dwindling congregation, sometimes no more than about a dozen people, and eventually Hope Chapel as such closed. The building is now the home of Hope Community church.

Lady Hope is not only commemorated by her eponymous church but also by several nearby streets: Hope Chapel Hill and Hope Square.

Hotwells Spa

The curious semi-circular building with pillars in front looking out across the River Avon at Hotwells is a reminder of the days when the wealthy and the fashionable flocked to the area. No longer do visitors come here to take the waters at the Hotwells Spa: instead they sit in seemingly endless queues of traffic outside The Colonnade.

The existence of a warm spring at the foot of St Vincent's Rocks had long been known but it was not until the seventeenth century that its water was claimed to cure such ailments as kidney diseases and diabetes. It had long been popular though with sailors as a cure for scurvy. Such was the fame of the spring that Hotwells and Clifton grew rapidly as tourist resorts. The visitors could stay in lodgings in the elegant houses that were being built on the steep hillsides climbing up into Clifton. Many of Bristol's glassmakers were kept busy producing bottles for the spa water which was being sent all over the world.

The spa attracted many of society's leading lights during its season, which ran from April to September, fitting in quite comfortably with the winter season at the much better known spa at Bath. Among the visitors to Hotwells were Charles II's Queen, Catherine of Braganza. From the literary set of the 1700s were the likes of writer and Whig politician Joseph Addison, the poet William Cowper and playwright Richard Brinsley Sheridan. However, the poet Alexander Pope did not think much of it saying 'I believe the Bristol waters at the Well, would be serviceable if I could stay long enough, viz. six weeks or two months'. The spa's decline was as fast as its rapid rise, after it was discovered that its healing powers may not have been as efficacious as once believed.

Behind the Colonnade's pillars at street level was an arcade of shops patronised by the visitors. Anna Yearsley, the Bristol milkmaid turned poet, is said to have run a circulating library there. Next door was Hotwell House with its pump room and baths built on a ledge jutting out into the River Avon. Hotwell House was demolished to make way

The Colonnade is all that remains of Hotwells' heady days as a spa.

for road development. The shops are no more but the Colonnade has been turned into homes which are still occupied.

Inns

Many inns, public houses, hostelries or taverns, call them what you will, are veritable treasure troves of a city's history. They are integral to Britain. In Chaucer's *Canterbury Tales* the pilgrims stopped at various inns and Charles Dickens wrote endlessly about them, including the Bush Hotel in Corn Street.

The Bush – a branch of Lloyds TSB now occupies the site – was where Mr Winkle took up his quarters in his 'love-lorn quest' for the missing Arabella Allen in Dickens' *Pickwick Papers*. It was here too that Edmund Burke, the eighteenth-century writer and philosopher and Member of Parliament for Bristol for six years, set up his election campaign headquarters.

The Bush was described as having 'so many bedrooms as might have lodged King Priam's sons-in-law'. It was also one of the city's principal coaching inns. Passengers were charged three pence a mile for the journey to London. In 1778 the Birmingham Post Coach service was inaugurated, with coaches leaving the Bush at five o'clock each afternoon.

The Rummer: the scene of much Bristol history.

One of the hotel's landlords, John Weeks, had a reputation for his lavish banquets. He advertised his turtles as being 'dressed daily'. They weighed anything from forty pounds to two-hundred weights. On Christmas Day, Weeks covered the 'great table with a glorious load of roast beef and plum pudding, flanked most plenteously with double home-brewed of such mighty strength and glorious flavour, that one might well have called it malt wine rather than malt liquor'. The festive menu included a baron of beef weighing 350 pounds, along with various delicacies ranging from swan to shrimps.

In All Saints' Lane off Corn Street, The Rummer, nestling in the hub of St Nicholas covered market, claims to be the city's oldest inn with a hostelry being on the site as early as 1241. Originally it was known as the Greene Lattis, apparently on account of the large use of that colour around the windows. When Thomas Abyndon, a warden at neighbouring All Saints' church, became landlord it traded as Abyndon's Inn. There were many other name changes but it has been The Rummer since 1743 when architect John Wood the Elder partly rebuilt it after working on the Corn Exchange.

It is hard to imagine that with all the events happening here patrons would be short of topics for conversation as they quaffed their ale. An impressive number of royal guests, including Elizabeth I, Charles I, Charles II and William III, are said to have either visited or stayed at The Rummer. One old newspaper cutting says that, around the sixteenth century, soldiers on their way to Ireland to stamp out a rebellion stayed here for six weeks when contrary winds prevented their ship from sailing. Poet Samuel Taylor Coleridge, author of *Kubla Khan* and many other poems, penned some of the issues of his radical magazine *The Watchman* here.

When John Palmer MP, a brewer from Bath, contracted with the General Post Office to carry mail by coach instead of post boys, The Rummer became a coaching house. The first coach carrying mail from London on 18 August 1784 arrived here shortly before midnight after a fifteen hour journey. However, the mails were transferred to the 'iron road' when the Great Western Railway opened in 1841.

Brothers Frank and Aldo Berni started a revolution at The Rummer in 1955 which changed a nation's eating habits. It was the first of the steak bars for which they became renowned. Their menu of traditional steak and chips was rolled out across Bristol and then the rest of the country. This enterprising duo soon had 150 steak bars, but the revolution died out in the 1970s when tastes changed again. This time Indian and Chinese restaurants started appearing on almost every street corner. Berni Inns were taken over by catering giant Grand Metropolitan and later sold to Whitbread.

Having been closed for several years The Rummer re-opened at the start of 2006 to quench the thirsts of its customers after another makeover. The pub takes its name from a large drinking mug called a rummer.

King Street

This cobbled street was laid out in the seventeenth century and named in honour of Charles II. It is sometimes referred to as Bristol's 'Museum Street' and is often said to be the most historic in the city with its architecture spanning three centuries. At one end are the quaint almshouses for retired merchant seamen and endowed by the Society of Merchant Venturers. Next door the Old City Library, founded in 1613, is now a Chinese restaurant. The poets Samuel Taylor Coleridge, Robert Southey and William Wordsworth were among those who frequented the library. Further along the street is the Theatre Royal, the oldest working playhouse in England. Its neighbour is the mid-seventeenth century St Nicholas with Burton's Almshouse.

On the other side of King Street is one of the city's best known pubs, the Llandoger Trow. This is one of Bristol's last timber-framed buildings, dating from 1664. This form

A nineteenth-century view of the Theatre Royal.

The Llandoger Trow, pictured before the Second World War.

of construction became obsolete after the Great Fire of London two years later. In the early days the Llandoger occupied only one of the five original gables. A grocer and a tobacconist were among the various traders that occupied the rest. The two end gables were blitzed during the last war. It is uncertain when ale was first dispensed here. However, the pub's unusual name is thought to derive from the industrial profile of the area in the seventeenth century when water-borne trade was carried out between Bristol and South Wales. Llandogo is a village on the River Wye, and the barges or two-masted vessels that plied their way between there and Welsh Back at the end of King Street were known as trows.

The pub is supposed to have been the setting for a meeting between the writer Daniel Defoe and Alexander Selkirk, who had been marooned on an island and was the inspirational figure behind *Robinson Crusoe*. Local legend also has it that Long John Silver met the hero of Robert Louis Stevenson's swashbuckling tale, *Treasure Island*, here. King Street's old inns now stand cheek by jowl with an outburst of twentieth century clubs and café-bars, but they still conjure up visions of the days of smugglers, press gangs and pirates.

Legal Eagles

Bristol is distinguished in having the oldest Law Society in the country. It was established in 1770 and is senior to the national Law Society by fifty-five years. The Bristol society's first meeting was held in the Bush Tavern, Corn Street, when eighteen founder members were present. They described themselves as 'practicers of the laws of this realm'. The society then consisted of barristers, practising attorneys and solicitors in Chancery.

One of its early rules stipulated that meetings should start at 'seven o'clock in the evening and continue until half an hour after ten when the Tavern Bill should be called for and discharged'. Another rule said that each member (residing in Bristol, or within five miles thereof) who was absent for the 'whole time' of any meeting 'shall forfeit Two shillings and Sixpence'. Members were also barred from introducing cards, dice or any other sort of game into the society.

From its inception the society met fortnightly and at each meeting the lawyers appointed one of their number to preside. Although the late eighteenth century saw a profusion of social clubs of all kinds, this society was unique in Bristol as being the only group of professional men who gathered to primarily discuss professional business. A highlight of the society's year was the annual dinner, a function that is still an important event in the solicitor's calendar.

Bristol Law Society now has hundreds of members and has cultivated links with legal associations throughout Europe. They now meet in the Law Library, a street or two away from the site of the old Bush Hotel and next door to the Crown Court.

The oldest surviving legal practice in England can, unsurprisingly, be found in Bristol too. Records show that the firm of Gregg Latcham and Quinn can trace its roots back to the 1690s when one Thomas Latcham was in business. He married in 1699 and on his wedding certificate he described himself as an attorney. Furthermore, a legal document witnessed by him in 1710 still exists.

The Law Library to the left of the Crown Court, Small Street.

The business was passed from father down to son, eventually reaching Charles Latcham, who was born in 1811. His sister married a Charles Montague and the Montagues inherited the firm, which stayed in their family until the 1920s. Through another marriage the Niblett family joined the business. Until the start of this century the firm worked out of offices in a Georgian building on Stokes Croft but moved to Queen Square into another Georgian building and became styled as Gregg Latcham Quinn. However, the Niblett family is still represented, with Edward Niblett being a consultant to the practice.

Lending Library

It has been around so long that Bristolians tend to take the Central Library for granted but the building itself is something of a treasure and reflects the city's long history of book lending. This dates back to 1613 when Robert Redwood, a wealthy merchant, gave his lodge in King Street for conversion into a library for 'the benefit of the citizens'. This was the second earliest free public library in England.

It got off to a good start thanks to the Archbishop of York, Dr Tobias Matthew, who remembered his native city and donated a large number of his books from his

Details from the frieze on the façade of the Central Library, College Green.

extensive library. Dr Matthew was born in a room above a shop on Bristol Bridge. He said his books were for the 'free use of the merchants and shopkeepers of the city'. The library has kept a letter that Coleridge wrote complaining about an officious librarian.

In 1740 the new City Library was built on the same site – now a restaurant – and its users included such famous literati as the Lake District poet Samuel Taylor Coleridge and the Bristol-born poet laureate Robert Southey. Sir Humphrey Davy, who started off his scientific career in Dowry Square, Hotwells, and is probably best known for his miners' safety lamp, was also a subscriber.

It was in 1902 that the old Bristol Corporation set up a competition to find a designer for the present library next to the cathedral. It was won by architect Charles

Henry Holden. His library was opened in December 1905 at a cost of £30,000. But the ratepayers did not have to find a penny because a public spirited citizen, Vincent Stuckey Lean, left £50,000 in his will for the 'erection of a new Reference Library'. Mr Lean, who died in 1899 aged seventy-nine, was a barrister who had devoted his life to the arts, literature, natural history and travel. He also bequeathed his collection of books to the new library. His life's work was a study of the world's proverbs.

With its sweeping marble staircase leading from the entrance hall to the first floor, the library soon won national acclaim for its design. Sir Nikolaus Pevsner, the art historian and architectural scholar, said this was Holden's 'most remarkable work before he started his chain of underground stations in London in 1932'. It was a remarkable accolade for an architect aged just twenty-seven.

The unusual frieze on the Deanery Road façade depicts twenty-one characters with literary connections. Among those carved in stone are seven saints including Cuthbert and Augustine. They are joined by the Venerable Bede and six members of the cast of Chaucer's *Canterbury Tales*. The frieze is the work of Bristol-born sculptor Charles James Pibworth. It was described by Pevsner as a 'favoured motif of progressive architects'.

On the first floor of the library is the magnificent and unique 'Bristol Room'. This is an astonishing replica of the King Street library as it was when Coleridge and other poets used it. A beautiful carved fireplace by Grinling Gibbons, along with panelling and shelves, were also removed to the present library.

Lord Mayor's Chapel

Nestling between the shops on College Green with its modest façade is the only church or chapel in England owned and maintained by a local authority, or in other words, the council taxpayers. This was originally a chapel for the Hospital of the Gaunts, founded in around 1220 by Sir Maurice de Gaunt and his nephew Robert Gournay to tend the sick, feed the poor and provide schooling for a dozen boys. It was dissolved when Henry VIII suppressed the monasteries in 1539. Shortly afterwards Bristol Corporation purchased it for £1,000 and ever since it has been under the control of the local authority.

For a while the chapel, officially dedicated to St Mark, provided a refuge for French Hugenots, exiled from France. It became the official place of worship for the Lord Mayor, councillors and aldermen in 1722 after they had an unusual falling out with the clergy at Bristol Cathedral. Apparently, the city fathers were in the habit of leaving services before listening to the sermon, which in those days lasted for an hour or more. In doing so they not only snubbed the preacher but also caused a commotion. Since then those responsible for civic affairs have attended St Mark's for prayers before meetings of the full council, before the ceremony of mayor-making each May and on some religious feast days, hence St Mark's being more affectionately known as the Lord Mayor's Chapel.

High Court judges, robed in red and bewigged, arrived by horse-drawn carriage for worship here before going on to dispense justice at the old Bristol Assize. The tradition fell by the wayside with the introduction of Crown Courts in 1974.

Above: *The Lord Mayor's Chapel,
College Green.*

Right: *All are welcome at the Lord
Mayor's Chapel.*

Many treasures can be found in the chapel including effigies of its founders in chain mail, beautiful medieval tombs, Flemish and French painted glass and post-reformation monuments. There is Baroque iron work by the eighteenth century Bristol craftsman William Edney, brought here from the bombed Temple church off Victoria Street. The Lord Mayor's Chapel is not just for use by civic dignitaries. All are welcome to visit or attend services there.

The Mansion House

Not many people build a house and then give it away. But that is just what Alderman Thomas Proctor did. After buying a plot of land at The Promenade, on the edge of Clifton Downs, in 1865, he appointed architects George and Henry Godwin to build a mansion for him. Two years and £2,500 later Elmdale House, a twenty-two room gentleman's residence, complete with spacious drawing room, galleries on the different floors, a lift from the kitchen to the dining area and a billiards room was ready for occupation. It was built with stone quarried on the spot, with Bath stone dressing.

This was Proctor's home for about seven years until in 1874 he announced his intention to give Elmdale House to the city on May 1, his wedding anniversary. The city fathers were surprised by his generosity and further taken aback when they discovered that Proctor's gift came complete with fixtures, fittings and furnishings as well as a cheque for £500 for repairs and decorations.

The gesture was typical of Proctor, who became wealthy through his chemical, manure and fertiliser business besides dealing in property. Amongst other benefactions he paid for the restoration of the North Porch of St Mary Redcliffe church. Although he was born in Birmingham, Proctor immersed himself in Bristol's civic affairs, becoming an alderman and High Sheriff. Ill health prevented him from taking up the office of Mayor. When he died in 1876 aged sixty-four, flags were flown at half mast on many public buildings.

Elmdale House became known as The Mansion House and to this day it is still the official residence of the Lord Mayor and Lady Mayoress of Bristol during their term of office. Many civic functions are held here and the city flag flies when the mayoral couple are in residence. Over the years various members of the Royal Family, including the Queen, the Duke of Edinburgh, the Princess Royal and the Duchess of Kent, have been welcomed here. Little could Proctor have dreamt that Bristol's 'No.1 address' would today probably carry a price tag of several million pounds.

Merchants' Hall

Of all the fine mansions on the broad sweep of The Promenade on Clifton Down, the Merchants' Hall is easily recognised by its brightly painted carved coat of arms. This is not one house though, but two knocked together, and is the headquarters of one of the city's most ancient and controversial organisations. The Society of Merchant

The entrance to the Mansion House.

Merchants' Hall, Clifton Down.

Venturers was founded by royal charter of Edward VI in 1552, although its origins date back to a thirteenth-century merchant organisation. Its original purpose was to secure a monopoly on overseas trade by merchants sailing from the port of Bristol.

This is an organisation which Bristolians seem to either love or loathe. Its members, the majority male, have long been accused of being a secretive cabal recruited from wealthy families with roots deeply entrenched in the area. There have also been claims, strongly refuted, that the society manipulates the life of the city behind the closed doors of its rather grand hall.

The original seventeenth-century Merchants' Hall stood near the corner of Marsh Street and King Street in the centre of the city until it was eventually destroyed in the Second World War. As a temporary move the society acquired Fern House, a large semi-detached mansion on The Promenade. Four years later the next door property, Auckland House, came on the market and the Merchants' combined the two to create a new hall, used for banquets, members' meetings and receptions.

Many historic portraits, royal charters and a saddle cloth which belonged to Elizabeth I when she rode into Bristol in 1574 are kept here. The blue velvet cloth was originally given to a High Sheriff but when it came up for sale in 1947 prominent Bristolian Sir Foster Robinson, twice the Society's Master, bought it and presented it to the Merchant Venturers.

The Society no longer looks after the port but its main job is now acting as trustee of endowment funds for several leading charitable organisations, including St Monica's home for the elderly at Westbury-on-Trym and schools endowed by the benefactor Edward Colston. It also helps community groups and provides volunteers to serve on Bristol University's decision making bodies and the city's Downs Committee.

Throughout its history the Society has invited various eminent people to become honorary members. They include the Duke of Edinburgh, and four Princes of Wales, the last being Prince Charles. A number of prominent statesmen including Edmund Burke, Winston Churchill and Margaret Thatcher are also on the honorary roll. The Merchants' court of officers still forms the executive body which is elected, along with a new Master and Wardens, on November 10 each year, a date which is set by a charter granted in 1639 by Charles I. The various elections take place in the Merchants' Hall.

St Michael's Hill

Walk by the church at the top of St Michael's Hill and you are treading on truly historic ground. The church stands on the site where five Marian martyrs were burned at the stake. Two memorial tablets, one inside and one on the outer wall of the church, tell of the death of the men between 1555 and 1557 for 'their avowal of the Christian faith'. A gallows was also erected here where murderers and robbers met their end.

The church opened for worship in 1843 as Highbury Congregational Chapel. It was intended for the families who were to move into the as yet unbuilt homes on the surrounding fields now known as Cotham. William Day Wills and his brother Henry Overton Wills, of the tobacco family, were the main benefactors. They put their faith in a young and unknown architect, William Butterfield, to design their chapel. He was, in fact, a nephew of the Wills brothers.

Cotham Parish Church.

Colston's Almshouse, St Michael's Hill.

The old Children's Hospital, St Michael's Hill.

For Butterfield, who was only twenty-eight, this was his first work and the only non-conformist chapel he was to ever build. He designed it in fifteenth-century Gothic style, although there were later additions, most notably the tower. Butterfield went on to become an outstanding ecclesiastical architect, building many churches and chapels, both at home and abroad, including those at Balliol and Merton colleges. Overseas he was responsible for cathedrals in Australia, India, Madagascar and South Africa. He died in 1900 aged eighty-six, having designed more than sixty churches.

Highbury Chapel became the Anglican parish church for Cotham in the mid-1970s. This landmark building stands at the top of St Michael's Hill, a thoroughfare steeped in history itself with many fine Georgian houses and offering panoramic views of the city. It was one of the ancient roads leading from Bristol to Wales via the ferry at Aust. The now redundant and rather neglected and vandalised church of St Michael the Archangel on the Mount Without stands at the foot of the hill. Its name reflects the church's position outside the old city wall. Originally built around 1148, it was remodelled in the fifteenth century and again around 1775. Ironically, its tower was the last symbol of Christian faith that those Marian Martyrs saw as they met their fate.

St Michael's Hill was one of the first roads outside the old city to have domestic buildings and some fine examples can be seen next to St Michael's church. On the opposite side of the road stands the Scotchman and His Pack, a pub which, unlike many others, has not changed its name for 150 years. It recalls the days when a wedge of wood was placed under the wheels of a cart to prevent it rolling backwards when a delivery was being made in hilly areas. A few doors up the hill is Colston's Almshouse, founded by Edward Colston in 1691, with its own chapel. Colston insisted that the twelve men and twelve women who lived there should be Bristolians and members of the Church of England.

On the brow of the hill is the now redundant hospital for children founded by a group of businessmen in 1866 in one room with nine cots. It began as the Bristol Hospital for Sick Children and Women. Queen Victoria permitted the prefix 'Royal' to be added in 1897. Treatment for women, however, ceased in the early years of the last war. Since then the hospital, now in a brand new £22 million building alongside the Bristol Royal Infirmary, has been known as the Bristol Royal Hospital for Sick Children. Much of the old building – save for the façade – is expected to be demolished to make way for a new School of Biological Sciences for Bristol University.

Muller's Orphanages

George Muller, who was born in Prussia in 1805 and came to Bristol when he was twenty-seven, became one of the city's greatest social reformers. He was concerned about children begging on the streets and with his wife he founded an orphanage in rented terraced houses in Wilson Street, St Paul's. This home provided room for about thirty children. The houses quickly became inadequate to meet the need so Muller decided to build an orphanage on the ridge in Ashley Down, in those days a rural area outside the Bristol boundary. His first property there opened in 1849 and was able to accommodate 300 children. Twenty years later there was a total of five houses costing more than £100,000. By then the Muller homes were caring for more than 2,000 young people.

Muller never appealed for funds but prayed for the money to carry out his work. Donations from the public came rolling in and it is said that during his lifetime Muller received more than £1 million. Besides paying for buildings the money also went on clothing and feeding the orphans.

With the passing of the Children and Young Persons Act in 1948, the Muller Homes became inadequate to meet modern requirements. The last of the orphanages closed ten years later and the Muller trustees sold the buildings to the old Department of Education, using the proceeds to buy and equip Family Group Homes. Bristol Technical College opened on the Ashley Down site in 1960, later becoming Brunel College and now known as the City of Bristol College. The five orphanges, along with swimming baths, became Grade II★ listed buildings in 1998 and the whole site was designated as a Conservation Area by the city council.

Muller also founded the Scriptural Knowledge Mission whose objectives included the foundation of Sunday Schools in the city and the support and maintenance of missionaries. When he died, at the age of ninety-two, the whole of Bristol stopped for his funeral. His estate was valued at just £160, reflecting the simple life that he led. Muller Road is named in honour of the philanthropist. The Muller Foundation still survives with its headquarters in Cotham.

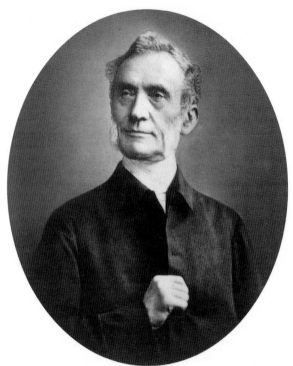

Right: *George Muller.*

Below: *An old postcard showing Muller's Orphanages at Ashley Down.*

New Gaol

The crumbling granite gatehouse with side towers standing on Cumberland Road overlooking the New Cut is all that remains of the New Gaol, at one time an extensive building. It checked in its first inmates in August 1820, having replaced Newgate Prison on the site of the Galleries Shopping Centre. The New Gaol could hold about 200 criminals and debtors and had a flat roof with a trap door for public hangings which were a popular spectator attraction.

The first public hanging at the gaol took place nine months later. Thousands of people (some accounts put the number as high as fifty thousand) gathered outside to watch the last mortal moments of eighteen-year-old John Horwood. The number of onlookers was so great that notices were displayed warning people about the danger of falling into the New Cut, which was unfenced at the time. Horwood was taken to the gallows after being convicted of killing his sweetheart. His trial was told that during a lovers' tiff Horwood had thrown a stone at the girl, injuring her skull. She died in hospital three weeks later.

In 1831, when Bristol witnessed what were then the worst civil disturbances in its history, the New Gaol was attacked by rioters. They had broken away from a much larger crowd in Queen Square protesting about the Reform Bill which was being debated in parliament. They breached the prison's iron gates after battering them with sledge hammers, hatchets and crowbars for three-quarters of an hour. A small boy was able to get inside and draw back its bolts. The inevitable happened and about 170 prisoners were freed and joined the mob. They set on fire the treadmill and gallows, along with the governor's house and the prison chapel. Order was eventually restored to the city by troops from Gloucester who opened fire on the crowd, killing around 130 of them.

The New Gaol was closed in 1883 when Bristol Prison at Horfield was opened and the land was sold to the Great Western Railway. For many years it was used as a coal yard. The little that is now left of the prison is to be incorporated into a new development of homes, offices and leisure facilities.

Newspaper Wars

The history of provincial journalism makes interesting reading, especially in Bristol, which was the battle ground for an intriguing newspaper war. It started in 1702 when *The Bristol Postboy*, the city's first ever paper, was published.

Just over 150 years later Bristolians were spoilt for choice with four weekly papers being printed on Saturdays with two more on Wednesdays. By the late 1920s, however, there were only three locally-owned papers hitting the news-stands: the *Bristol Evening News*; the *Bristol Times and Mirror* and the *Western Daily Press*. Only the latter, which has been chronicling local affairs since 1858, survives.

The remains of the old Cumberland Road gaol.

The *Evening News* and the *Times and Mirror* found in 1932 that they were in financial difficulties with falling circulations because of fierce competition from the fledgling *Evening World*. This was owned by the 1st Viscount Rothermere and first appeared on the streets of Bristol in 1929. Although it was directed from London the *World* was printed in a purpose-built newspaper office, Northcliffe House on Colston Avenue. With its illuminated clock on a tower set above the central entrance the building is still a distinctive sight but is now trendily renamed Colston 33. The *Evening News* folded, and Lord Rothermere later bought out the shares of the *Times and Mirror* and closed the paper down. The façade of its offices, in the style of the arts and crafts movement, with the paper's name carved in stone, remains untouched in narrow St Stephen's Street, off the city centre. The interior has been converted into a hostel for backpackers.

Bristolians did not take lightly to what they saw as the intrusion of a London-owned publication which was running many promotional stunts to boost circulation. In one, the *World* offered a five-shilling book of National Savings Stamps if you ordered the paper for ten weeks. There was strong feeling that the city should have its own newspaper and the Bishop of Malmesbury, who lived at Stoke Bishop, supported by leading businessmen launched an appeal to find the necessary funds to start one. The result was the *Bristol Evening Post* which rolled off the presses for the first time on 18 April 1932. Among the original 900 shareholders were many who had invested just £1. The generosity of Bristolians in providing capital of nearly £42,000 gave rise to the slogan: 'The Paper all Bristol asked for and helped to create'. Those words appeared on the first edition and are still printed today at the top of the paper's leader column.

Right: *A promotional postcard showing the offices of the* Bristol Times & Mirror *and the* Bristol Evening Times. *The exterior of the building in St Stephen's Street remains untouched.*

Below: *The old* Evening World *offices, Colston Avenue.*

After a row with the rival *Evening World* and a subsequent truce, *Bristol United Press* was formed to run both papers and in 1962 the *World* and *Post* merged. By then the *Evening Post* had also taken over the ailing *Western Daily Press* printed in Baldwin Street. It brought in a Fleet Street journalist to turn its fortunes around.

For more than forty years the *Evening Post* was printed in a disused leather warehouse – now a building society office – in Silver Street on the edge of Broadmead. But by 1975 the cramped red-brick building was no longer suitable for a fast expanding newspaper empire. A custom-designed press hall with offices above, clad in purple brick and tile, was built on Temple Way.

Newspaper history took a dramatic and ironic turn in 1998 when the *Post*'s shareholders – then mainly large institutions – yielded to a takeover bid from Rothermere's group. It means that the paper Bristol fought so hard to put in place is itself now a wholly-owned Northcliffe paper.

Observatory and Camera Obscura

The round stone-built tower which stands on the site of an ancient British camp overlooking the Clifton Suspension Bridge must be one of Bristol's most unusual buildings. Strategically placed on the city's highest point at 338ft above sea level it was originally a windmill, known as the snuff mill. It had been built by James Waters in 1776 on land that he leased from the Society of Merchant Venturers. It was his family home until the mill was burnt down two years later, the sails having been overdriven in a gale.

The mill remained derelict until 1828 when local artist and amateur astronomer William West rented the ruins for five shillings a year and rebuilt them. West not only lived there but also used the tower as a studio, and converted the former windmill into an observatory. He installed a telescope, a wind gauge, and astronomical instruments as well as fixing a camera obscura with five inch diameter lens and mirror to the top of the tower. This still reflects a 360-degree panoramic view of Clifton taking in the Avon Gorge, Clifton Suspension Bridge and even people passing by, onto a white 5ft diameter bowl-shaped viewing table in a darkened room below. An old advert said that 'to the unaccustomed the camera obscura has a magic effect and affords a high gratification to the observer'.

The entrepreneurial West then set about blasting and boring the hard limestone rock beneath the observatory to create a passage to St Vincent's Cave. Originally the only access was by way of a steep and perilous path down the cliff face. William Wyrcestre the fifteenth century Bristol-born writer recorded that it took him '124 paces to reach the cave'. The story goes that the cave was connected with an ancient chapel and hermitage called St Vincent as pieces of carved masonry were found there. West spent £1,300 excavating the 200ft long tunnel and building a viewing platform – still a popular tourist attraction – on the sheer face of the Avon Gorge.

He died in 1861 but his relatives continued to live in the observatory until 1943. Since then it has been sold by the Merchant Venturers and at the start of 2006 was undergoing a privately financed restoration programme.

The Clifton Observatory and Camera Obscura on Clifton Down.

Old City Wall

St John's Arch at the bottom of Broad Street with a church perched above is another of the city's more unusual historical features. This is the only surviving gateway – there were once nine – which protected the walled town in the Middle Ages. It was through this arch with its portcullis that Elizabeth I entered Bristol on horseback in 1574 and received an address of welcome at this spot. The two brightly painted dumpy statues either side of the arch are said to represent Brennus and Belinus, legendary Roman founders of Bristol.

The church, dedicated to St John the Baptist, is small and narrow having been built on the city wall and is peculiar in that it has no east or west windows. There has been a place of worship here since the twelfth century – its founder was a Mayor of Bristol – with the present building having been restored in 1825. Churches were often built on walls at a city exit as favoured locations for travellers' prayers before a journey. St John's street level crypt has been put to many uses, including that of a storehouse for sugar and acting as an auctioneer's room. During wartime it served as an air-raid shelter.

On the outer side of the city wall in Nelson Street is St John's Conduit, built in the fourteenth century to bring water from a spring near the top of Park Street. During the Second World War it came into its own, supplying water to this part of the city after bombs fractured the pipes of the water authority mains. St John's church is now redundant but visitors are welcomed at certain times. Around the corner, the back wall of the one-room White Lion public house on the Quay Head is actually part of the old city wall. It can be seen through an internal panel.

Old Council House

The office of Lord Mayor of Bristol sounds as old as the city itself. But Bristol has only had a Lord Mayor since 1899. Previously its Leading, or First Citizen, was a mere Mayor. The first of this long line was Roger de Cordwaner in 1216 and the last was Herbert Ashman in 1898.

Queen Victoria granted Bristol the power to elect Lord Mayors and in 1899 on her first visit to the city as Queen – just two years before her death – she knighted Mr Ashman on the steps of the Old Council House in Corn Street. He then served as First Citizen for a second year – but this time with the much grander title of Lord Mayor. This is the gift of the monarch and only about two-dozen cities in the country have been honoured with it.

The Old Council House on the corner of Corn Street and Broad Street was first built in 1551, replacing St Ewen's church, and has twice been remodelled. Above the entrance can be seen the work of local sculptor, Edward Hodges Baily, with his figure representing Justice. Inside, the Old Council House resembles an art gallery with many fine large paintings depicting scenes from Bristol's history including Cabot leaving the harbour for Newfoundland. The paintings were commissioned by local businessmen as a gift to the city.

Belinus is one of the mythical Roman founders of Bristol.

St John's archway, the only surviving gateway of the old city wall.

Aldermen and councillors met here to run civic affairs and proclamations were often delivered from the Council House steps. Several thousand people thronged here for the Lord Mayor's celebration speech, made from the city's magnificent horse-drawn Proclamation Coach, at the end of the Second World War. With the expansion of local government it was decided in 1934 that a much larger building was needed as the city's administrative headquarters. Plans were drawn up for a new Council House on College Green, the foundation stone of which was laid in 1938. But the war and the national economic situation afterwards interrupted construction work. It finally got the royal seal of approval when the Queen officially opened the crescent-shaped brick-built offices in April 1956 on her first visit to the city as monarch. Such has been the rapid growth of local government down the years that the new Council House was soon found not to be big enough for all the council's departments. Overflow offices had to be built alongside.

Civic history can be seen in the list of Mayors and Lord Mayors from 1216 to the present day in the Conference Hall. Their names and dates of their terms of office are carved in stone on the wall. The ceiling of the council chamber is painted with scenes from local history and the Lord Mayor's Parlour has much civic insignia. From the central archway of the Council House a symbolic figure of an Elizabethan seaman looks out across College Green.

Meanwhile, the Old Council House has served a number of uses. In recent years it has provided overflow accommodation for the Law Courts, and has been refurbished as the new home for the Register Office for births, marriages and deaths which has moved from the thirteenth-century Quaker's Friars.

Paying on the Nail

The unusual four brass pillars, or nails, standing outside the Corn Exchange in Corn Street are a reminder of how business was carried out long before the introduction of credit cards and electronic cash transfers. It was here that merchants met for business and probably used the nails for the exchange of money to settle their deals. The flat tops of the nails with their raised edges would have prevented coins falling onto the pavement.

The nails originally stood under a covered walkway known as the Merchants Tolzey, on the north side of All Saints' church. When alterations were made to the paved area around the Tolzey in 1771 the nails were moved to their present site. They are still used, albeit once a year, for their original purpose. Every November the presidents of the Colston Societies, each wearing top hat and tails, meet here to exchange cheques. This brief ceremony marks the launch of the societies' respective annual appeals for funds to help their work with the needy. The phrase 'pay on the nail' may well have originated from the Corn Street cash transactions. However, the nails are not peculiar to Bristol.

The Stag and Hounds housed the ancient Pie Poudre Court.

Pie Poudre Court

From the twelfth century onwards a large market serving Bristol Castle was held on what is now Old Market Street, one of the city's widest thoroughfares. Markets and fairs were common all over England attracting not only merchants, traders and buyers from far and wide but also a motley collection of rogues, thieves and debtors, who travelled around, too. The pickings of these thieves would doubtless have been rich with the many hundreds of people milling around the stalls. In Norman times a court was set up to deal swiftly with the felons who plagued the market. Justice was dispensed so quickly that it was known as Pie Poudre Court, from the Norman 'dusty feet'. The story goes that justice was meted out so swiftly that defendants had no time to shake the dust off their shoes and disappear.

The court was originally held in the open air under an old oak tree but later moved into the Stag and Hounds public house. The first official records of a pub on the site date back to 1815, although the premises were built during the seventeenth century, probably as a private home. Unfortunately, no record can be found of when the court moved indoors.

Pie Poudre Court was wound up in 1870 but it became a tradition to ceremonially open the proceedings of the court under the portico of the Stag and Hounds on 30 September each year. All those having business with the court were invited to step forward by the Town Crier and a proclamation was read. This brief ceremony was abandoned in 1973 following a government review of the court system throughout the land. It seems that the only record of Bristol's Pie Poudre Court is now a small wooden sign outside the pub giving the briefest of details about this fascinating chapter in legal history. The panelled first-floor room where the court sat is still there and so is a Jacobean seventeenth-century staircase. An 80ft deep well discovered during a refurbishment of the pub in 1986 is now a feature of the bar.

Poet's Place

Standing beside traffic-choked Redcliffe Way is the façade of the school attended by the boy poet Thomas Chatterton, who arguably is more famous for dying young than for anything he wrote. Behind this façade is Chatterton's birthplace. He died in a London garret three months short of his eighteenth birthday, after an overdose of drugs. Chatterton had fled his native city in despair because his literary genius had gone unrecognised.

This son of a schoolmaster spent much time in St Mary Redcliffe church opposite his home. He was fascinated by inscriptions on graveyard monuments and in old parchment documents that he found in the church's muniment room. This, apparently, fired his imagination and he adopted the persona of a fictitious scholar and monk whom he named Thomas Rowley. Chatterton wrote glittering epic poetry in fake medieval English which he then attributed to Rowley. For a while he was able to fool the public, including many respected literary figures, into believing them genuine.

The Chatterton story itself triggered an industry devoted to commemorating him. The poets Wordsworth and Coleridge wrote about him; a French dramatist scripted a play on Chatterton while a German composer produced an opera about his life. Artists have depicted his death on canvas, and many academic books and even a novel have been written about him, as well as television documentaries and a stage play.

Chatterton became the hero of the Romantic movement but Bristol has remained largely indifferent to him. His birthplace was in the way of a 1930s road-widening scheme – its original site is now a surface car park – so it was removed a few hundred yards to stand in pointless isolation in Redcliffe Way. A memorial to the poet – a statue of a boy dressed in a Colston School tunic – was taken down from Redcliffe churchyard in 1967. In recent years a Bristol University academic, Dr Nick Groom, found remains of the monument covered by a paper sack in a shed behind Chatterton's home. The only memorial inside the church is a small plaque bearing the simple inscription 'Thomas Chatterton of this parish 1752-1770 Poet'. A statue of the boy was erected in Millennium Square in 2000.

Chatterton may well have written his poetry more than 200 years ago but members of the Thomas Chatterton Society around the world are doing their best to ensure it lives on. Its secretary, Dr Groom, is adamant that the city should make more of its most famous poet, perhaps opening a museum dedicated to him. 'He was prodigiously gifted

Thomas Chatterton's birthplace stands in virtual isolation. The façade of the school he attended stands at the side of the house.

and could have lived for another fifty years. There is no indication that had he lived he would not have continued writing,' said Mr Groom.

Queen Square

This is the city's biggest and most graceful square with some fine Georgian buildings around the sides. It was laid out on a muddy marsh in 1700 and named in honour of Queen Anne, who visited Bristol two years later on her way to Bath where she was taking the waters to relieve her gout. This small part of Bristol has been the scene of important events that have become the stuff of history.

The Reverend John Reade, Vicar of St Nicholas' church beside Bristol Bridge, built the first house in 1700. It formed one of the corners of the eastern side of the planned square. One of the sheriffs followed suit and Queen Square quickly became a fashionable residential area. It was described by a contemporary writer as 'an agreeable place of habitation, as well as a resort in fine weather for gentlemen and ladies'.

Queen Square.

William III on horseback has pride of place in Queen Square.

Queen Square from the air.

One of its residents was the naval adventurer and privateer Captain Woodes Rogers. He is best known for finding the sailor Alexander Selkirk, who was left marooned on the island of Juan Fernandez in the South Seas for four years after a dispute with his captain. Woodes Rogers brought Selkirk to Bristol and his remarkable story inspired the eighteenth-century writer Daniel Defoe to create his novel *Robinson Crusoe*. Rogers wrote a volume about his own voyages, which mainly consisted of piracy.

A pioneer in renal medicine, Richard Bright, was born in Queen Square in 1789. He published his findings on the kidney disease named after him – Bright's Disease – and at the beginning of Queen Victoria's reign he was appointed Royal Physician Extraordinary.

It was in Queen Square that the first American consulate in Europe was opened in 1792. This became a popular consular centre, with Belgian, Finnish, German, Greek, Italian, Dutch, Portugese and Spanish representatives based here in the 1960s. The old Port of Bristol Authority, along with many shipping firms, had their headquarters in the square. Officials of the Wills tobacco firm came here daily to hand over cheques at the Customs House for excise duty on tobacco being taken out of the bonded warehouses. Modern technology put an end to this routine with the introduction of electronic transfer of payments.

Many of Queen Square's imposing buildings, including the Mayor's Mansion House, were destroyed by fire during the Reform Riots of 1831 and had to be rebuilt. In 1936 the square was blighted when the city council carved a dual carriageway diagonally through it, linking Broad Quay with Redcliffe. However, that was removed during

St Mary Redcliffe Church.

a regeneration scheme which started in 1998 and was designed to restore the square to its former glory. The council's City Centre Projects and Urban Design Team won numerous accolades for this scheme, including national awards from the Royal Town Planning Institute and Civic Trust. In the latest edition of Pevsner's architectural guide to Bristol the restoration is described as 'visionary'. Some of the offices around the square are now being turned back into residential accommodation.

Queen Square is dominated by a statue of William III in Roman costume on horseback. It was cast in brass by the Dutch émigré Michael Rysbrack. The Grade I★ listed statue was put in place in 1736 at a cost of nearly £2,000. When the Second World War broke out the statue was taken down from its plinth and moved to Badminton Park, Gloucestershire, the home of the Duke of Beaufort, for safekeeping.

St Mary Redcliffe

Although it is a parish church, St Mary Redcliffe is often mistaken for a cathedral, no doubt because of its grace and space. So much of the history of Bristol has taken place within its walls and countless national and international figures have been associated with it or paid visits to the church. This masterpiece of Gothic architecture, completed in the late fifteenth century, has been lauded by monarchs, praised by poets, captured on canvas by many an artist and pictured on postcards aplenty.

The armour and pennants of Admiral Sir William Penn.

St Mary Redcliffe was traditionally the church visited by seafarers leaving and returning to the medieval port of Bristol. The north porch was the 'Seafarers' Shrine' which sailors could visit when the main door was closed. In the church itself there are reminders of Bristol's maritime past including the rib bone of a whale said to have been brought back from John Cabot's voyage to Newfoundland in 1497. It now rests near a model of his ship *The Matthew*. On the wall of the tower is a memorial to Admiral Sir William Penn, described by contemporary writers as the most distinguished Bristolian of the seventeenth century. He led the victory over the Dutch and French fleets in the English Channel. Penn died in London but left instructions for his remains to be buried

St Mary Redcliffe: 'the most famous and fairest parish church in the land.'

in Redcliffe church. His son, also William, became the founder of the Quaker colony of Pennsylvania. William Canynges, a rich fifteenth-century merchant and ship owner, is commemorated by a stained glass window and also two tombs. Figures of John Cabot and his three sons with his tiny ship, *The Matthew*, appear in the same window. There is a brass monument to John and Joanna Brook. Joanna was the daughter and heir to Richard Ameryck, after whom America may be named.

The ceiling is a vast vault of stone ribs and more than a thousand bosses, beautifully carved by medieval masons. They were originally painted in many colours but were gilded in the eighteenth century. At about the same time the Lady Chapel temporarily became the home of the parish school which had been founded in 1571. The wooden benches on which pupils sat are still in the church. Queen Elizabeth I granted 'Letters Patent' to the vestry of the church, allowing a free grammar and literature school for boys of the parish to be founded.

Men of words and music also feature prominently in Redcliffe's history. Handel, a personal friend of a one-time vicar here, is commemorated in a window which has the unusual feature of extracts from a musical – eight selections from the *Messiah*. The boy-poet Thomas Chatterton is remembered by a small plaque, and the poets Samuel Taylor Coleridge and Robert Southey, the Poet Laureate, married two sisters here within a month of each other in 1795.

The landmark spire, rising to 292ft above street level, has not always been there. During a storm in 1446 two thirds of it toppled across the nave and the church was left with a truncated tower until reconstruction work was completed in 1882. Interestingly, the builder of the spire used the same techniques in scaffolding as those in the fourteenth century.

But for all its history, stunning architecture and tradition St Mary Redcliffe is not simply an ancient monument, its clergy acting as curators guiding curious visitors around the tomb stones, wall plaques and effigies. There has been a place of Christian worship on this site since AD1115 and nearly 900 years on people still meet here to pray, study and worship God. It is a venue for baptisms and weddings, a place of farewells and a focus of celebration, hope and prayer.

Rocks Railway

There is something unusual at the foot of the Avon Gorge rock face near Bridge Valley Road. Carved out of the limestone cliff is the Hotwells entrance to a railway which no longer takes anyone anywhere. Thousands of people once used the Clifton Rocks Railway which linked Clifton to the pleasure steamers calling at Hotwells, the train to Avonmouth or the trams into the centre of the city. It was a water-powered funicular railway like that at Lynton and Lynmouth in North Devon, but there was a big difference. This one was in a tunnel bored through solid rock.

It was an ambitious scheme promoted by George Newnes, Member of Parliament for Newmarket and founder of Newnes Publishing Company, who had a country home near Lynmouth. The railway in a tunnel idea was conceived to protect the spectacular visual impact of the Avon Gorge, also noted for its wealth of wildlife. It took two years to excavate the 500ft long tunnel (climbing at a vertical rise of 1ft for every 2.2ft), install

The Clifton Rocks Railway at the end of the nineteenth century.

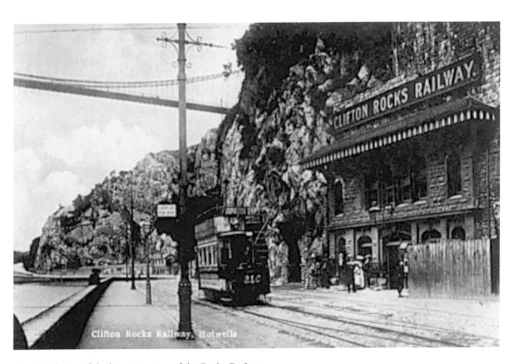

A postcard view of the lower terminus of the Rocks Railway.

The Clifton Rocks Railway. 291.

Left: *One of the four cars of the railway.*

Below: *A later view of the Rocks Railway, with windows bricked up.*

the track, the four carriages and build stations at both ends. The job took twice as long as expected and the bill of £30,000 – being solely financed by Newnes – was three times the estimated cost.

On the opening day, 11 March 1893, more than 6,200 people passed through the turnstiles for the return journey. At the end of the first six weeks the management reported that the railway was so popular that it had carried more than 100,000 passengers. By the end of the first year of the railway's operation that figure had risen to 427,492. The railway certainly reduced travelling time for passengers, climbing up through the gorge to Clifton in just forty seconds.

In 1908 the firm that ran the railway went broke and it closed. However, four years later George White, the Bristol pioneer of electric tramways and aviation, re-opened the railway as part of his tramway system. By the 1930s though, trade had fallen off so much that the railway was finally closed in 1934. The four carriages were lowered to the Hotwells station and later removed. During the Second World War the tunnel became a secret transmission base for the BBC.

Until 2005 the top, or Clifton, station next to the Avon Gorge Hotel was a derelict triangular building, but a band of enthusiastic volunteers are busy with the major challenge of clearing debris and restoring it. They would like to re-open the railway and link it up with a ferry service running from Hotwells into the centre of Bristol: a project which they say could cost anything between £15 and £20 million. Whether this fascinating part of Bristol's history can be repeated remains to be seen.

Royal York Crescent

Eugenie House at the western end of Clifton's grand Royal York Crescent takes its name from Eugenie de Montijo. She was the daughter of a Spanish nobleman who was sent to learn English at a small boarding school for young ladies on the crescent. Eugenie tried to flee the school but was found on board a ship in the docks bound for India. She married Napoleon III in 1853 and was Empress of France from then until 1870. She died in this country at the age of 94.

The young Eugenie lived in Royal York Crescent, reputed to be the longest in Europe, not long after it was completed in 1820 having taken some thirty years to build. Work started on the crescent in 1791 to a design by the Bristol architect William Paty, but was brought to a standstill by the bankruptcy of the developer, with just a quarter of the houses completed. The developer's downfall came during a depression in the property market caused by the Napoleonic wars.

The building site had been standing idle for eight years when the War Department bought the ground and the unfinished part of the crescent intending to build barracks. However, local opposition frustrated this plan and the crescent was completed in 1820 as originally envisaged. The builders may have had something of a superstitious streak about them for the crescent does not have a number 13. Instead, they numbered one of the properties as 12a. At one time the crescent had its own beadle and outsiders were not encouraged.

Most of the houses have now been converted into flats but plaques on the exterior of some of them recall the days when famous people had their homes there including Sir

Above: Royal York Crescent, Clifton.

Below: A plaque on one of the houses on Royal York Crescent.

SIR·ABRAHAM·ROBERTS.G.C.B.
A·DISTINGUISHED·INDIAN·GENERAL
LIVED·IN·THIS·HOUSE·FOR·MANY
YEARS·AND·DIED·HERE·ON
DECEMBER·28TH·1873.
HIS·SON
FIELD·MARSHAL·EARL·ROBERTS
K.G. K.P. G.C.B. V.C. ETC
ALSO·LIVED·HERE·IN·HIS·EARLY·LIFE

ERECTED·BY·THE·CLIFTON
IMPROVEMENT
COMMITTEE·

Abraham Roberts, one of Britain's great generals. After joining the East India Company and fighting in the first Afghan wars he retired to live at Royal York Crescent where he died in 1873, aged seventy-nine. His son, the hero of Kandahar, unveiled the plaque on his father's home. Eugenie House won a Civic Trust award for its 'sensitive conversion' into providing accommodation for retired people.

Rush Sunday

There's a chance to see a colourful bit of Bristol history being re-enacted at St Mary Redcliffe every Whit Sunday, or Pentecost as it is known in the church calendar. This is when the church, reputedly described by Queen Elizabeth I as 'the fairest, goodliest and most famous parish church in England,' holds its Rush Sunday Service.

This unusual tradition started when William Spencer, one time Mayor, desirous it seems of getting more people to church, made provision in his will for sermons to be preached to the Mayor and commonalty on three days at Whitsun. Spencer died in 1493 and the first Rush ceremony at Redcliffe was held the following year. As far as can be discovered from parish and civic records, it seems that the pattern of the service has changed little down the centuries, save that the three sermons have been cut to one. This is believed to have happened at the time of the Reformation. The preacher, usually Redcliffe's vicar, is paid the equivalent of 6s 8d, the amount specified by Spencer in his will. An added perk is that he is invited by the Lord Mayor to lunch at the Mansion House afterwards, again in keeping with the instructions in Spencer's will.

Rush Sunday is the most spectacular event in Bristol's calendar of ceremonial events. The Lord Mayor, aldermen and councillors attend the service in State, their scarlet robes bringing a splash of colour to the spring morning. The Lord Mayor arrives in an open horse-drawn carriage escorted by mounted police. His entry into the church is heralded by a fanfare sounded by the liveried City Trumpeters whose office dates back to the seventeenth century. Preceding him is the City Sword Bearer wearing his Cap of Maintenance – a furry Cossack-style affair from Elizabethan times,

Numerous dignitaries including the Lord Lieutenant, the High Sheriff of Bristol, Crown Court judges and the local coroner can be seen processing around the outside of the church before the service. Most of them are wearing costumes that would not look out of place in a Gilbert and Sullivan opera. As they make their way to the pews they tread over a carpet of rushes, freshly picked from the Somerset moors. A nosegay, or posy of herbs, believed to have warded off foul smells in olden times, is placed in front of their seats. All this is in keeping with ancient tradition. This is the oldest surviving Rush ceremony of its kind in the country that can be traced with any certainty.

Sculptor Extraordinaire

To discover some of the gems of Bristol's architectural history you need to crane your neck and look upwards. That certainly needs to be done to appreciate the work of the

The Rush Sunday nosegays.

The frieze above the entrance to the Freemason's Hall, Park Street, is one of the many works of Edward Hodges Baily.

sculptor Edward Hodges Baily. His most famous statue is that of a one-eyed and one-armed Admiral Nelson which stands on the top of Nelson's Column in Trafalgar Square, but there is still plenty of his work to be seen in Bristol.

Baily, the son of a ship's carver, was born in Downend in 1788 and educated at Bristol Grammar School, which he left when he was fourteen years old. He was placed in a merchant's counting house where he stayed for two years, occupying spare moments by modelling likenesses of friends in wax. Bailey was still in his teens when he moved to London and became a pupil of John Flaxman, the first Professor of Sculpture at the Royal Academy. Baily was quickly acclaimed as a sculptor of genius and before he was twenty he had carried off a prize given by the Society of Arts. A year later he was awarded the first Silver Medal of the Royal Academy, followed by its much-coveted gold medallion and a cash award of fifty guineas – regarded as the blue riband of the RA at the time.

Baily's services were much in demand by royalty. George IV commissioned him to produce some of the decorations for Buckingham Palace and Queen Victoria asked him to carve a bust of Prince Albert. He produced numerous portrait busts and monumental statues of leading figures of the day, from politicians to poets and from painters to scientists. They can be seen in various parts of the country. Baily's bust of the Bristol-born Poet Laureate Robert Southey can be found in the north choir aisle of Bristol Cathedral. Elsewhere in the city he carved the classic frieze above the entrance to the Freemason's Hall – originally the home of Bristol Philosophical and Literary Institution – at the bottom of Park Street. His statue of 'Justice' stands above the entrance to the Old Council House. Bristol Museum and Art Gallery displays his 'Eve at the Fountain', one of the most famous pieces of British sculpture in the nineteenth century. The marble for this cost him £400.

Baily, who married when he was eighteen, had two sons and two daughters. He died in London in 1867. Although his work was widely acclaimed, with one London newspaper describing him as 'the greatest of modern sculptors', Bristol seems to have forgotten him. There are no signposts spotlighting his work or memorials for him.

Shot Tower

The Lead Shot Tower is a prominent landmark beside the Floating Harbour at St Philip's. It has been a feature of the skyline since 1968 when it replaced the world's first tower specifically designed for making lead shot. The St Philip's tower ceased production in 1995 and a decade later the 150ft high building was converted into offices.

Shot was made in the city for more than two centuries after William Watts is said to have had a dream in which he envisaged making it in completely spherical form. This was achieved by pouring molten lead from a height, through a perforated drum into a water-filled pit. Lead shot was much in demand by the military for their muskets, and by farmers shooting pests, but the pellets available to them were uneven and pockmarked.

Watts, a plumber by trade, put his dream to the test and in 1782 took off the top of his home on Redcliffe Hill opposite St Mary Redcliffe and built a square castellated tower some 50ft high. He made holes in the floors and excavated a pit in the basement.

The Shot Tower that stood on Redcliffe Hill for nearly two centuries.

The result was smooth lead shot. Watts patented his process and eventually sold his business for £10,000. However, he quickly lost his fortune when he dabbled in property development in Clifton and became bankrupt.

The story of Watts' dream may well be the stuff of legend but lead shot was made on Redcliffe Hill until 1968. Although Watts' tower was officially designated by the government as being of historical importance and therefore a 'listed building' it was nevertheless demolished. It was pulled down to allow Redcliffe Hill to be turned into a dual carriageway.

A small plaque recalling this remarkable chapter in Bristol's industrial history can be found on an empty office block on Redcliffe Hill.

The replacement tower in St Phillips.

Sugar House

A modern hotel in the centre of the city would seem to be the most unlikely of places in which to find links with an industry that was thriving in eighteenth- and nineteenth-century Bristol. But the Hotel du Vin has been developed in an old Sugar House and has retained some of its features.

Sugar was one of the principal commodities traded through the port of Bristol. Sugar refining started in the city early in the seventeenth century. By the middle of the nineteenth century around a dozen sugar refineries were in business. However, fifty years later there was little left of the industry, it now being centred on Bristol's rival ports of London and Liverpool.

When the sugar arrived from the plantations in the Caribbean it was the job of the refiners to remove impurities and produce various grades of pure white crystalline sugar. This labour intensive process was carried out at various locations in Bristol, including the site of the Hotel du Vin in Lewins Mead. The first sugar house here was built in 1728. It was redesigned when steam engines were developed to speed up production at the end of the eighteenth century and a boiler room, chimney and engine house were added. Despite all the changes the sugar house closed as a refinery in 1831.

Since then the building has been used and reused and redesigned many times. It was initially converted to houses and later became a warehouse for tobacco, and after that stored bird seed before being converted into offices. The old Sugar House was left empty and derelict, with much of the structure rotting for around fifteen years until 1999: it was at the top of the 'buildings at risk' register run by Bristol City Council. At that time the building was once again the focus for another transformation, this time into a hotel. During a £4.5 million conversion the developers kept the Sugar House's 100ft high chimney in the middle of the courtyard. It now makes for an interesting feature in the hotel's reception area and a wine cellar has been created in the old engine room of the sugar refinery.

Swimming Pool

Tucked away in the labyrinth of narrow streets behind Clifton's Victoria Rooms is the Victoria Open Air Pool, the UK's oldest such Grade II★ building. It opened as a private subscription bath, initially for men only, at six o'clock on the morning of 19 July 1850. Admission cost one shilling per person which included the use of two towels. It was another twenty-one years before women were welcomed.

Open air pools or lidos – so called after the island bathing beach near Venice of that name – were all the fashion before swimming at the beach came into vogue or public baths were provided by local authorities. The Victoria Pool was eventually taken over by Bristol's council in 1897 from private ownership. *Chilcott's Guide to Bristol* of 1909 said 'the establishment is admirably conducted. The baths are supplied by Bristol Water Company and the swimming bath is capacious'. Sixty-seven years later the first edition of another guide book, *Children's Bristol*, recorded that the city council ran nine swimming pools spread across the suburbs, but 'one of the most popular' was Clifton's open air pool in Oakfield Road. Indeed it was! In 1976, when the sun blazed all summer, attendance on one day peaked at a record 6,000.

The turnstiles were locked for the last time in 1990 when the council said that the cost of repairing a bad leak and relining the pool was prohibitive. The pool was drained and the site has since fallen into a sad state of disrepair. Over the last fifty years some 300 lidos have closed in this country but swimming alfresco is now making a comeback with local communities rediscovering the value of their heritage. A local businessman has now drawn up ambitious plans to revive the Clifton lido and intends to add a café, restaurant and other facilities expected of a twenty-first century leisure complex.

Clifton Open Air Pool, waiting to be given a new lease of life.

The ruins of Temple Church, off Victoria Street.

Temple Tower

It looks as if it will topple down on the small shops at its base at any moment: the tower of Temple church is 5ft out of true at the top on the west face. But then it has been like that for more than 500 years. This is Bristol's answer to the Leaning Tower of Pisa.

The church was founded by Robert, Earl of Gloucester *c.* 1147 when he made a grant of the land to the Knights Templar, a society of soldier monks formed during the Crusades. The original building was of circular plan, but it was replaced during the fourteenth and fifteenth centuries by the present structure when the church was given to the Knights of St John and a parish was formed for people living nearby.

Work on the tower started in the fourteenth century but during construction the foundations sank. Efforts were made to throw the 113ft tower back but were unsuccessful. The tower was completed in 1460.

During the Second World War this was one of eighteen Anglican churches across the city that was destroyed by incendiary bombs. Only the shell of Temple church was left, but rather curiously the tower withstood the bombs and fires that raged all around. The story is often recounted by Bristolians who lived through the war that a soldier had to be dissuaded from demolishing the tower for safety reasons, believing that enemy action had made it a dangerous building. The tower is not open for viewing but the shell of Temple church off Victoria Street can easily be seen. Some of the church's treasures, especially of plate and brass, were transferred to St Mary Redcliffe.

References to the Templars can be found in various nearby road names like Temple Way and Temple Street and, of course, in Temple Meads railway station, as well as the newly developed commercial quarter of Temple Quay.

Shops in Temple Street in the early 1900s.

The Theatre Royal. To its left is Coopers' Hall and to the right St Nicholas' Almshouse, which still stands.

Theatre Royal

The Theatre Royal in King Street has the proud distinction of being the oldest working theatre in the land. The curtain went up for the first time in 1766 but not without protests from the Society of Friends which was very much anti-stage. But the theatre's manager fought off the opposition by advertising the first production as a 'concert of Musick and a Specimen of Rhetorick', which turned out to be the usual services of the theatre orchestra with a comedy and a farce. A first night poster stated quite bluntly: 'No rowdy elements admitted'. The actor David Garrick wrote the prologue for the first play and he later described the theatre as the 'most beautiful theatre in Europe'.

The fifty original proprietors of the Theatre Royal who each subscribed £50 towards the cost of the building were given a silver token. Each one was inscribed with the words: 'The proprietor of this ticket is entitled to the sight of any performance to be exhibited in this house'. A further forty-seven people each gave £30 to the cost but did not receive a perk.

Twelve years later the playhouse got the royal seal of approval when it was recognised by George III as the 'Theatre Royal'. Right from the beginning to the present day many famous actors, such as Sarah Siddons, Ellen Terry and Henry Irving, have trod the boards at King Street. The ghost of Sarah Siddons is said to still haunt the theatre.

In 1942 the theatre was offered for sale by auction, but an appeal for funds, launched from the stage, saved it for the people of Bristol. It was bought by the Theatre Royal Bristol Trust, which four years later invited the London Old Vic to set up a resident repertory company. This became known as the Bristol Old Vic, still the resident company in King Street but long independent of its London tie. The company included a cast of actors which critics described as 'star-studded' – Peter O'Toole, John Neville, Timothy West, Barbara Leigh-Hunt and Dorothy Tutin, to name a few.

It was also in 1946 that Laurence Olivier officially opened the Bristol Old Vic Theatre School. This started life around the corner in Queen Charlotte Street but has since moved to a much larger building overlooking Clifton Downs. Such is the school's reputation that students enrol from all over the world. It not only provides training for acting students but also courses for designers and technicians.

The Theatre Royal's first major redevelopment in 200 years came in 1972 when it acquired its next-door neighbour, the eighteenth century Coopers Hall. Originally a guild hall for the city's many coopers, and at the time a storehouse for fruit and vegetables, it was incorporated into the theatre. This meant that the Old Vic could build a second studio theatre called the New Vic. Until then access to the main theatre was via a long dingy corridor, but that was replaced by the present modern foyer.

Tobacco Bonds

Bristol was one of the places where Sir Walter Raleigh is reputed to have smoked the first pipe of tobacco in England. We shall never know if that was true or not, but the city did become one of the United Kingdom's most important centres of the tobacco industry. Tobacco leaf arrived from Canada, East Africa and India as well as America. At one time over a fifth of the total imports of tobacco into the United Kingdom passed through Bristol's port. .

After it arrived at Avonmouth Docks the tobacco was taken by lorry and barge to the bonded warehouses upriver in Bristol. Three of the bonds dominated the skyline at Canons Marsh for sixty years. They were built in 1920 to store tobacco leaf, which was only released on the payment of excise duty by the cigarette manufacturers to Customs and Excise collectors. Each bond consisted of a reception area, sorting and delivery floor and nine storage levels.

But with the regeneration of Canons Marsh those gaunt tobacco bonds were spectacularly blown up early on a Sunday morning in the spring of 1988. It was the biggest explosion Bristol had experienced since the war. Lloyds Bank had taken over the site to build a £90 million administrative headquarters where staff from London would be relocated.

Three other bonded warehouses are still standing on the edge of the Cumberland Basin, although they now have uses far different from that originally intended. These bonds of red and blue brick were built between 1908 and 1920 for the old Port of Bristol Authority. Taken altogether these bonds and those at Canons Marsh gave the port a total storage capacity for more then 150,000 casks of tobacco leaf. One of the Cumberland Basin warehouses – B Bond – is now the home of the city's Record

The bonded warehouses dominated Canons Marsh.

Going, going, gone... the tobacco bonds disappear in clouds of smoke during a controlled explosion.

Office, where archives of local history going back many centuries are stored. More than £600,000 has been spent on converting another bond into ten floors of individual storage units.

Tramline Horror

A tram line partly buried in the churchyard of St Mary Redcliffe not only serves as a reminder of the dreadful horrors of war but also as a memorial of a public transport system that carried passengers across the city for more than forty years. The electric tram service came to an end on the night of 11 April 1941 when a bomb fell on Halfpenny Bridge next to the generating station at Counterslip, severing the power supply to all the vehicles.

In the same air raid another bomb fell on Redcliffe Hill shortly before midnight, ripping apart shops, homes, offices and the road itself. Such was the force of the blast that it uprooted part of a tram line at the junction of Redcliffe Hill and Guinea Street. This piece of iron was hurled several hundred yards over burning rooftops, eventually embedding itself in the south churchyard of St Mary Redcliffe.

Canon Sydney Swann, Vicar of Redcliffe at the time, made a note in his diary: 'How high it went into the air (the tramline) I have no idea. I remember thinking "that tramline must remain. It will be of interest."' Five feet of the track stands at a precarious angle in the manicured lawn, but no one knows how much is buried in the earth. This was the closest the church had come to serious wartime damage. Canon Swann also noted: 'The eleventh of April 1941 was the only occasion that we had a really large bomb on Redcliffe Parish though of course, there were many smaller ones and still more incendiaries.'

Some people said it was a miracle that St Mary Redcliffe had been spared, pointing out that its cloud-piercing spire standing sentinel-like on the edge of the city docks must have been a prime target for enemy bombers. Others said that it was testimony to the work of Canon Swann, who led a band of lads (firewatchers) over the church roof to deal with incendiaries and clear gutters after each air raid. A contemporary report said that the vicar did this 'with all the enthusiasm of a rugger player'. Canon Swann recruited the firewatchers from his congregation after exhorting them: 'If this national treasure is burned, when it could have been saved, how will we feel about it and what will England, and more than England, think of us?' Damage to the church was largely confined to the loss of irreplaceable medieval stained glass. The spire also suffered some blast damage when a High Explosive bomb fell on what is now the traffic roundabout outside the church.

Underfoot Bristol

Mention caves and most minds are likely to conjure up a vision of prehistoric man eking out an existence by hunting small mammals and wearing clothing made from strips of pelts and marsh plants. Bristol has its own caves, a honeycomb of them under the Redcliffe

A curious memorial in St Mary Redcliffe Churchyard.

area. But these are not thought to be a natural feature formed by running water. Instead, they are believed to be man-made, being excavated between the fifteenth and eighteenth centuries. Writing on the walls dating back to 1761 has been discovered by members of the Axbridge Caving Group, which has more than a half a century's experience of exploring the caves below the Mendip Hills. Pick marks have also been identified on the walls and ceilings and several artefacts have also been unearthed. The largest of the caverns is 45ft in diameter and 7ft high with a vaulted roof supported on eight columns at equal distances with a ninth in the centre of the space. They extend some two or three acres beneath Redcliffe but it is thought there are more caves to be discovered.

Red sandstone rock from the caverns was probably turned into sand and used in Bristol's one-time flourishing glass-making and pottery industries around the Redcliffe and Temple areas. It was also used as ballast for ships.

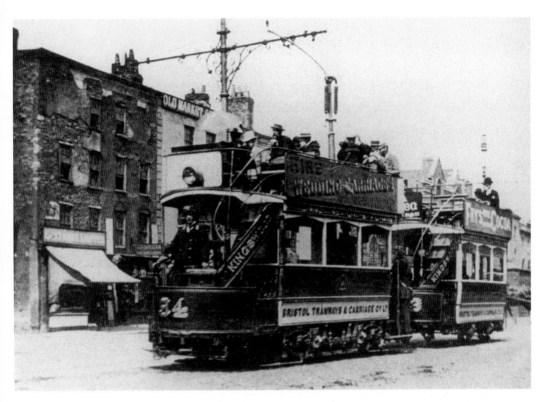

The tram from Kingswood arrives in Old Market Street.

Down the years the caves have been used as storage space for waste disposal from the glass works and from William Watts Lead Shot Tower, which stood on Redcliffe Hill. During the early part of the Second World War one of the smaller caverns was fitted with bunk beds and became an air-raid shelter for the families living along nearby Redcliffe Parade. Popular folklore has it that slaves were kept in chains here, and at one time smugglers secreted their contraband here, but no evidence has ever been found to support either theory. Redcliffe Caves are now one of the biggest tourist attractions on Bristol Doors Open Day each September, when the public are invited into buildings normally closed.

A small cave hewn out of the sandstone rock at the foot of Redcliffe Hill housed St John's Hermitage. It was here in 1346 that Thomas, Lord Berkeley placed one John Sparkes, a hermit, to pray for him and his family. It is known that the cave was still inhabited in the second half of the seventeenth century. A memorial tablet on an inside wall is inscribed with the legend: 'Here lyeth the body of Christopher the monk or Christopher Birchhead of this city mariner who died the 16th day of the 8th month in 1669'. Fronting the hermitage is an enclosed garden, formerly the burial ground for the Society of Friends (Quakers). Friends were laid to rest there between 1665 and 1923. The Friends gave the garden to the citizens of Bristol in 1950 and it is now maintained by the city council. The remains of the dead were re-interred at Avon View Cemetery but their tombstones can still be seen stacked up in the entrance to the hermitage.

THE ANCIENT REDCLIFF CAVES, BRISTOL, about which little is known, the passages extend for miles under the city, and have not been thoroughly explored.

Flash light photo FRED LITTLE.

Redcliffe Caves.

Water Maze

In this country we take water for granted but there was a time when it was a luxury. We are reminded of those days by keeping our eyes firmly focused on the ground in Victoria Park, Bedminster. This is where a fountain, built in brick in the design of a maze and surrounded by trees and grassland, links the Middle Ages with the present day. This unusual water feature, which was installed in 1984, has a lengthy inscription around it commemorating 'the recognition of the need for clean water.....by citizens of Bristol in both the twelfth and twentieth centuries.' The maze is notable for having no dead-ends and is a replica of a medieval roof boss in St Mary Redcliffe church, which can doubtless lay claim to being the smallest maze in the country, if not the world!

Victoria Park's maze serves as a fountain for an outlet of a water supply given to the church in 1190. It was then that Lord Robert de Berkeley, Lord of the Manor of Bedminster, gave the inhabitants of the growing hamlet of Redcliffe a water supply. It was piped from his 'Rugewell' on a hilltop at Knowle to a spout outside the church. This was the only source of fresh water the people of Redcliffe had for half a century. Lord Robert de Berkeley's gift was typical of the ancient endowments of the English church and it is Redcliffe's oldest known benefaction.

The Redcliffe water maze in Victoria Park, Bedminster.

Since time immemorial it has been the custom for the Vicar of Redcliffe, his churchwardens and parishioners to walk the course of the pipe, just over two miles, to lay claim to certain endowments. No ordinary trek this, for it starts at the well-head, now finding itself surrounded by dozens of allotments, off Daventry Road, and follows a route taking in pastureland, pavements, even a private garden, and Victoria Park to finish at a handsome bronze outlet on Redcliffe Hill. This monument was given to the church in 1931 and replaces the original water spout, believed to have been sited in nearby Pump Lane. It is inscribed with the Latin words of the original charter, which roughly translated mean 'For the health of the soul of Robert de Berkeley, who gave to God and to the church of Saint Mary Redcliffe and its ministers the Rugewell and its conduit'.

First-timers on what is known as the 'Pipe Walk' are ceremoniously bumped on a marker stone near the maze in Victoria Park. In the early years of the twentieth century the Pipe Walk was something of a rather grand affair. The *Western Daily Press* reported that the walkers were rewarded with a dinner in a marquee in the churchyard with music provided by local entertainers. It was thought that 'people who had trouble for a long walk should benefit of a comfortable confection afterwards'. Now they have to make do with a cup of coffee and a sticky bun.

Water ran the full length of the pipe until 1941 when it was damaged by incendiaries that dropped on Redcliffe Hill and the aptly named Spring Street during the Bristol

The outlet for the Redcliffe water pipe which can be seen on Redcliffe Hill.

blitzes. From time to time there has been talk of repairing the pipe but the cost has proved to be prohibitive.

W.D. & H.O. Wills

A red brick building with an imposing copper dome which dominates East Street is one of the few signs that this little bit of Bedminster was once the centre of Britain's tobacco industry. Indeed, it was the home of the largest tobacco factory in Europe, giving work in its hey day to around 6,000 people. Between them they were turning out some 350 million cigarettes every week. Statistics like these make it hard to believe that tobacco was once a banned import in Bristol. London had the monopoly of the trade until 1639 when the Privy Council revoked a long standing order that tobacco should only be shipped into the capital.

It was in 1786 that Henry Overton Wills, son of a clockmaker from Salisbury, Wiltshire, settled in Bristol and founded the tobacco business bearing his family name. An early factory was opened in Redcliffe Street. By 1830 Henry's sons, William Day Wills and Henry Overton Wills, were running the business. To meet the fast-growing

The Wills tobacco factory dominated East Street, Bedminster, for nearly a century. Parts of the arched frontage have been incorporated into an arcade of shops. A supermarket now occupies a large part of the site.

demand for cigarettes the firm moved into purpose-built factories down the road at East Street in 1884. It was here that one of Wills' most popular cigarette brands, the 'Wild Woodbine', was first made in 1888. Its green packet was a familiar sight on tobacconists' shelves well into the 1950s.

Bristol was fortunate in having such patrician employers as the Wills family. From the early days they were some of the most enlightened bosses in the land, setting up everything from dental and medical services to a savings bank and a library for their staff. One member of the family even invited workers to join him at home for Sunday lunch. A job at Wills was not only a good start in life but also regarded as a job for life. Generation after generation of the same family, largely from the closely-knit communities of Bedminster and neighbouring Southville, took home a Wills pay packet.

Not only did the tobacco barons look after their workforce but they were also generous benefactors across Bristol, founding not only its university but also building more than two-dozen churches, the city art gallery and museum, St Monica's Home on the Downs and many other fine public buildings.

The firm was on the move again in 1976 when the Bedminster factories became too cramped. This time the move was to a new £15 million factory on a greenfield site of nearly sixty acres at Hartcliffe on the southern edge of the city boundary. The move meant that Bedminster quickly became something of a ghost town. The owners of dozens of family shops that lined both sides of East Street, relying for years on Wills workers for their livelihoods, found the tills were no longer ringing. Shutting up shop for the last time soon became inevitable. Some of the East Street tobacco buildings were demolished to make way for a supermarket but the façade of the 1884 No.1 factory and two other sections have been retained. The frontage has been converted into an arcade incorporating a rank of small shops.

Thousands of Wills workers and their families suffered a major blow in 1991 when the Hanson Trust, then owners of the business, closed the Bristol factories and moved production to other parts of the country. It meant the end of a 200-year-old chapter in Bristol's industrial history.

Wills Memorial Building

No Bristolian can now imagine Bristol without its majestic Wills Memorial Building towering over the centre of the city from the top of Park Street. This mock-Gothic tower might well be the centre-piece of the University of Bristol's campus but it is also a memorial to one man. It owes its origin to two brothers, Sir George Wills and Mr Henry Herbert Wills, who wanted to mark the generosity of their father. It was a gift of £100,000 from Henry Overton Wills that enabled University College, as it then was, to be granted its charter in 1909 and become the University of Bristol. He also founded the university's professorial chairs of Greek, Mathematics and Physics.

A well respected local architect, George Oatley, was commissioned to build the monument. His design was inspired, apparently, by a dream in which he saw a tower on a hill with shields all around it. Once he got down to his drawing board in his tiny office in Orchard Street, off the bottom of Park Street, Oatley took just three weeks to come up with his design – and that was only working at nights. His plan was to

The Wills Memorial Tower.

provide around fifty rooms in addition to the magnificent Great Hall, used for degree ceremonies each February and July, a library, reception room and council chamber. He gave the imposing entrance hall an impressive twin staircase. It was all topped by a fan-vaulted ceiling which was assembled stone by stone. Oatley surmounted his tower with an octagonal belfry.

Construction work on the Wills Memorial Building started in 1914 but was interrupted by the First World War. Work resumed in 1919 and the tower was completed in 1925. It cost £501,566, well over the original budget of £100,000. On the side of the tower are nine shields representing well known Bristol families, including, of course, the Wills. Oatley was knighted for his work and the university recognised this too, conferring on him an Honorary Doctor of Laws degree. Thousands of Bristolians turned out on a burning hot June day for the official opening of this masterpiece in twentieth century craftsmanship by King George V and Queen Mary.

During the Second World War blitzes on Bristol, the university's Great Hall was badly damaged by an incendiary bomb. Another member of the Wills family, Lord Dulverton of Batsford, formerly Sir Gilbert Wills, obtained enough oak for restoration work to begin in 1959. The task was so great that it was another four years before the Great Hall was restored to its almost original splendour.

Bristol's largest bell, Great George, weighing nearly ten tons, sounds the hour from the top of the tower and tolls the death of monarchs and university chancellors. It was cast at a foundry in Loughborough and it was so big that two lorries were needed to bring it to Bristol. When it arrived after a twenty-four hour journey, it took a further sixteen hours to lift the bell into position. Great George is only manually swung on special occasions like the centenary birthday of the late Queen Mother, on her death in 2002 and again on the death of Diana, Princess of Wales in 1997. Great George is the sixth largest bell in the country.

The university as we know it today, carrying out major research into physics, medicine, engineering and veterinary science, was developed out of a series of educational successes. University College, founded in 1876, was the first institution in the United Kingdom to offer places to women to study in higher education on the same footing as men. The Bristol Medical School of 1833 became associated with the college, later becoming part of it. In 1909 University College combined with the Merchant Venturer's Technical College to become the University of Bristol. It was granted a royal charter by King Edward VII.

Zion House

Thousands of commuters pass Zion House every day but are probably unaware of its unusual history. This imposing building stands in its own grounds beside one of Bristol's busiest roundabouts, the dual Bedminster Bridge traffic system.

It was originally built as a church following a promise made by twenty-one-year-old John Hare in 1773. He had set out from his family home at Crowcombe, at the foot of the Quantock Hills in Somerset, to make his way to 'big brother Bristol' where he hoped to make his fortune. When he arrived at Bedminster, then a small rural haven made up of farms and meadows, he slept in an orchard. On waking the next day, John

Zion House, Bedminster, originally a chapel.

Hare vowed that should he become a wealthy merchant he would build a chapel on the very spot where he had rested.

He walked on into Bristol where he found a small shop to rent in Little King Street. It was big enough for his first experiments in printing floorcloth. However, business quickly expanded, forcing him to look for larger premises. John Hare took out a patent on his floorcloth and moved to a factory at Temple Gate.

It was fifty-six years later that his dream of building a chapel became a reality. He was now wealthy enough to buy the plot of land from Bristol Corporation. Part of his contract with the corporation stated that he was to 'erect a good and substantial chapel thereon for the worship of Almighty God by Protestant Dissenters of the Independent Denomination'. The foundation stone was laid by John Hare's wife on 12 May 1829. It took just a year for the chapel, with cast iron balcony and seating for 850 people, to be constructed. Zion Congregational Chapel held its first service on 15 June 1830 having cost John Hare £4,000.

By then the population of Bedminster had grown to 13,000. Church-going was an important part of family life and Zion's Sunday school had 600 youngsters on its register. Four months after the chapel opened John Hare signed it over to a group of trustees, numbering twenty-four in all, including his son, John. The latter was then running his father's lino business.

John Hare senior lived for another nine years to see his church well and truly established. He died at his home in Knowle, then in the County of Somerset, aged eighty-seven, and was buried in Zion Chapel. However, after his wife's death, John's remains were exhumed and re-interred at Arnos Vale cemetery so the couple could be buried together.

Zion Chapel's pillared portico and pediment remains unaltered to this day although the interior has been converted to provide district offices for Bristol City Council staff.

Zoo

The list of founders of Bristol Zoo reads like a *Who's Who* of eminent Bristolians in the Victorian era. There was Isambard Brunel, members of the Wills tobacco and Fry's chocolate families and the prominent Sturge Quaker family along with the Duke of Beaufort. Several hundred people paid £25 each for their stake in the menagerie. The amassed funds meant that the Bristol, Clifton, and West of England Zoological Society could buy a dozen acres of farmland on the edge of Clifton Downs in 1837 to develop their pet project. Some of the descendants of the original shareholders are still connected with the zoo, enjoying the benefit of free admission.

It is the fifth oldest zoo in the world and second oldest in Britain after London, and was opened with the aim of promoting 'the diffusion of useful knowledge' and 'affording rational amusement and recreation to visitors'. Apart from the animals the zoo's owners provided tennis and croquet courts, bandstand concerts, skating, tennis and archery for visitors to enjoy. Fetes and carnivals boosted income but such events were dropped in the 1920s so that the zoo could concentrate on research and breeding.

One of its founders, Dr Henry Riley of Clifton, said to be the first medical practitioner in the West Country to use the stethoscope, was the zoo's first secretary. Ever since, there have been close ties with the medical profession. Indeed, some surgeons at Bristol Royal Infirmary have even operated on animals and on one occasion two baby bears were admitted to the old Bristol Children's Hospital on St Michael's Hill suffering from pneumonia.

During the Second World War many of the animals were evacuated to safer areas although in the event this corner of Bristol escaped damage. The zoo itself played its part in helping others less fortunate. Its pavilion was taken over by staff from the Bristol Aeroplane Company after Filton was bombed, and the Clock Tower Restaurant became a canteen for American soldiers based at Clifton College next door. As part of the war effort the zoo authorities turned over the flower borders to vegetable plots.

Some of the residents became popular attractions for the thousands of visitors each year. Zebi the elephant was a talking point between 1868 and 1909 because of her propensity for removing and eating straw hats worn by visitors. Undoubtedly, the best-known inhabitant was Alfred the gorilla. He was bought for £350 and lived at Clifton from 1930 until he died in 1948. At the time he was the only gorilla in captivity in the country. From the moment he arrived Alfred was an instant success not only with the staff but also with visitors often meeting them on his walks around the grounds – accompanied by a keeper – wearing his distinctive woolly jumper.

Bristol Zoological gardens, Clifton.

Picture postcards of him were sent all over the world, many of them from American servicemen based in Bristol. Such was Alfred's fame that he even received greetings cards on his official birthday – September 5th. During his time at Clifton he gained so much weight that a special weighing machine had to be installed at the zoo. At one time Alfred tipped the scales at just over 26 stones.

When Alfred died zoo officials announced that his death was caused by a low-flying aircraft that made him panic. However, unknown to his many admirers he had been suffering from TB for a year.

In more recent years the zoo has developed its educational and scientific roles and is planning to create a £50 million zoo on a 130 acre site in south Gloucestershire where rhinos, giraffes and other exotic species will roam free. But the memories of Alfred live on. Taxidermists stuffed him and put him on display at Bristol Museum where he can still be seen. A bust of Alfred can also be found outside the zoo's Ape House.

Other local titles published by Tempus

Bristol Times revisited

DAVID HARRISON

This book is a collection of some of the articles drawn from the first year of the Bristol Times Supplement of the Bristol Evening Post. Each extract recalls an aspect of the city's lively, and sometimes turbulent, history. From tales of fairs, workhouses, riots and gaols, to accounts of star appearances at the hippodrome and the success of Fry's chocolate factory, each piece provides an insight into Bristol's past.

0 7524 2844 6

The Dings and St Philips

DAVID STEPHENSON AND JILL WILMOTT

This volume provides a glimpse into the history of The Dings and St Philips during the last century. Compiled with over 200 images, this selection highlights some of the changes and events that have taken place in these once industrious Bristol suburbs. Aspects of everyday life are also recalled, from shops, pubs and places of worship to celebrations and local sporting heroes.

0 7524 3556 6

Bristol Cinemas

DAVID STEPHENSON AND JILL WILMOTT

Through the medium of old photographs, programmes and advertisements, this book provides a fascinating look at the history of cinema-going in the city of Bristol and its suburbs during the last century. From mobile cinemas to penny gaffs, this A–Z of cinemas in Bristol chronicles the places frequented by Bristolians over the years, including the ABC on Whiteladies Road, the Magic Box in Stokes Croft and the Picture House in Knowle.

0 7524 3669 4

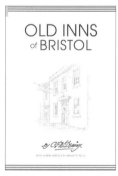

Old Inns of Bristol

CFW DENING, WITH A NEW PREFACE BY MAURICE FELLS

Old Inns of Bristol is a fascinating guide to the historic pubs in the city. First published in 1943, the original book is reproduced here, along with an updated preface by local writer and broadcaster Maurice Fells. This book offers the reader an insight into the life of pubs past and present, from the oddly named Rhubarb Tavern to the dockside pubs with their stories of pirates and smugglers.

0 7524 3475 6

If you are interested in purchasing other books published by Tempus, or in case you have difficulty finding any Tempus books in your local bookshop, you can also place orders directly through our website

www.tempus-publishing.com